The Bathroom Golf

ALMANAC

Compiled and edited by: Steve Heldt

Significant others:
Jack Kreismer   Geoff Scowcroft
Ellen Fischbein

Cover and Page Design:
Fred and Diane Swartz

RED-LETTER PRESS, INC.

Saddle River, New Jersey

JANUARY 1st

TODAY'S THOUGHT: "A game in which one endeavors to control a ball with implements ill adapted for the purpose." —*Woodrow Wilson, on golf*

HISTORY: On this date in 1938 the USGA, in an effort to speed up play, decreed that a player could use no more than 14 clubs.

QUIZ: Name the first golfer to win the U.S. Open and the British Open in the same year.

Chip Shot

A golf ball with no dimples will fly approximately 60 to 80 yards, taking off like an ordinary dimpled ball, but dropping quickly back to earth.

QUIZ ANSWER: Bobby Jones, who won both tournaments in 1926

JANUARY 2nd

TODAY'S THOUGHT: "If profanity had an influence on the flight of the ball, the game would be played far better than it is."

—*Horace Hutchinson, "Hints on the Game of Golf", 1886*

HISTORY: On this date in 1995 amateur golfer Sonya Osugi scored two holes-in-one during the same round at the Chung Shan Hot Springs Golf Club in southern China. Osugi was playing with a 24-stroke handicap.

QUIZ: What is Fuzzy Zoeller's real name?

Chip Shot

The odds of an amateur golfer recording a hole-in-one are approximately 43,000 to one.

QUIZ ANSWER: Frank Urban Zoeller, hence the nickname Fuzzy

The Bathroom Golf Almanac

JANUARY 3rd

TODAY'S THOUGHT: "Golf is an awkward set of bodily contortions designed to produce a graceful result." —Tommy Armour

HISTORY: On this date in 1991 Paul Azinger shot a bogey-free round of 67 to win the Pebble Beach National Pro-Am and the $198,000 first prize.

QUIZ: Who holds the record for most PGA tournaments won in a year?

Chip Shot
In 1457 the Scottish Parliament banned golf. The august body felt the time would be better spent practicing archery for defense against the English.

QUIZ ANSWER: Byron Nelson won 18 times in 1945.

JANUARY 4th

TODAY'S THOUGHT: "If you aspire to be a champion, it's up to you to find a way to get the ball in the cup on the crucial holes on that last day." —Tom Watson

HISTORY: On this date in 1973 the LPGA began its most ambitious season to date with a total purse of more than $1.5 million for 36 scheduled tournaments.

QUIZ: The PGA Tour record for winning the same event the most times is eight. Who holds the record?

Chip Shot
The highest score for one hole in a pro tournament is the 23 Tommy Armour carded on the 17th hole in the 1927 Shawnee Open.

QUIZ ANSWER: Sam Snead won the Greater Greensboro Open eight times.

JANUARY 5th

TODAY'S THOUGHT:

"Golf is absurd, stupid, ridiculous, impossible, unfair and wonderful." —*Art Spander, writer*

HISTORY: On this date in 1990 21-year old Robert Gamez was given the last spot in the Northern Telecom Open field. Gamez took advantage, winning his first-ever pro event the following weekend.

QUIZ: Who was the first American to win the British Open?

Chip Shot

The first time admission was charged for the U.S. Open was in 1922, when the price of a ticket was one dollar.

QUIZ ANSWER: Walter Hagen, in 1922

JANUARY 6th

TODAY'S THOUGHT: "It is this constant and undying hope for improvement that makes golf so exquisitely worth the playing." —*Bernard Darwin, writer*

HISTORY: On this date in 1957 Nancy Lopez was born. Lopez dazzled the golf world in 1978, winning 9 tournaments.

QUIZ: Lee Trevino has won three of the four majors in his long career. Can you name the only title to elude him?

Chip Shot

Golf is a game in which the slowest people are in front of you, and the fastest are behind you.

QUIZ ANSWER: Trevino has never won The Masters.

JANUARY 7th

TODAY'S THOUGHT: "Golf is not, on the whole, a game for realists. By its exactitudes of measurement it invites the attention of perfectionists."
—*Heywood Hale Broun, writer*

HISTORY: On this date in 1993 Fred Couples won his second consecutive award as the PGA Tour's Player of the Year.

QUIZ: Only two golfers have won PGA tournaments in four decades. Name them.

Chip Shot

1954 was the first year that women players could wear shorts in USGA-sponsored championships.

QUIZ ANSWER: Sam Snead ('30's — '60's) and Raymond Floyd ('60's — '90's)

JANUARY 8th

TODAY'S THOUGHT: "The sport isn't like any other where a player can take out all that is eating him on an opponent. In golf it's strictly you against your clubs." —*Bob Rosburg*

HISTORY: On this date in 1972 Brandie Burton was born. Burton joined the LPGA Tour in 1991 and won her first major tournament at the duMaurier Classic in 1993.

QUIZ: Who was the first golfer from Great Britain to win The Masters?

Chip Shot

Charles Sands of the United States won the first Olympic gold medal in men's golf at the 1900 Paris Olympics.

QUIZ ANSWER: Sandy Lyle, a Scot, won it in 1988.

JANUARY 9th

TODAY'S THOUGHT: "Serenity is knowing that your worst shot is still going to be pretty good."
—*Johnny Miller*

HISTORY: On this date in 1994 Phil Mickelson beat Fred Couples in a playoff, but Jack Nicklaus stole the spotlight at the Mercedes Championships. Nicklaus came from three strokes back to win the senior section of the event.

QUIZ: Who was the first amateur to win the U.S. Women's Open?

Chip Shot

Tommy Armour coined the term "yips" to describe the tension afflicting the nervous putter.

QUIZ ANSWER: Catherine Lacoste of France, in 1967

JANUARY 10th

TODAY'S THOUGHT: "Golf does strange things to other people, too. It makes liars out of honest men, cheats out of altruists, cowards out of brave men, and fools out of everybody." —*Milton Gross, writer*

HISTORY: On this date in 1992 TV caught Paul Azinger removing a leaf, costing him a two-stroke penalty at the Tournament of Champions.

QUIZ: During the 1980's I was the only player to win two PGA Championships. Who am I?

Chip Shot

President Dwight D. Eisenhower had a putting green installed outside the White House.

QUIZ ANSWER: Larry Nelson, who won in 1981 and 1987

JANUARY 11th

TODAY'S THOUGHT: "No man living can make a player keep his eye on the ball, and still this is the underlying secret of successful play."
—*Francis Ouimet, U.S. Open champion*

HISTORY: On this date in 1970 Billy Casper became the second golfer in history to win one million dollars in his career with a victory at the LA Open. Arnold Palmer was the first.

QUIZ: What pro golfer is known as "The Walrus"?

Chip Shot

The United States named their Ryder Cup squad in 1942 in case the war would end before the next scheduled match in 1943.

QUIZ ANSWER: Craig Stadler

JANUARY 12th

TODAY'S THOUGHT: "If you travel first class, you think first class and you're more likely to play first class." —*Raymond Floyd*

HISTORY: On this date in 1992 Steve Elkington sank a 10-foot birdie putt on the first extra hole to win the Tournament of Champions. Brad Faxon had rallied from two strokes down to force the playoff, only to fall short in the end.

QUIZ: Name the father and son who won 8 of the first 12 British Opens.

Chip Shot

The sand wedge was invented by Gene Sarazen in 1932.

QUIZ ANSWER: Tom Morris, Sr. and Tom Morris, Jr.

JANUARY 13th

TODAY'S THOUGHT: "Golf, like measles, should be caught young, for, if postponed to riper years, the results may be serious." —*P.G. Wodehouse, writer*

HISTORY: On this date in 1985 Otto Bucher became the oldest golfer to score a hole-in-one when he aced the 12th hole of the La Manga Golf Course in Spain. Bucher was 99 years old!

QUIZ: What is the name of the trophy given to the LPGA player with the lowest scoring average for the year?

Chip Shot
Arnold Palmer, the general of "Arnie's Army", served in the Coast Guard from 1951 to 1954.

QUIZ ANSWER: The Vare Trophy

JANUARY 14th

TODAY'S THOUGHT: "Golf is not a game of great shots. It's a game of the most accurate misses. The people who win make the smallest mistakes."
—*Gene Littler*

HISTORY: On this date in 1941 Senior PGA Tour player Gibby Gilbert was born. Gilbert earned over one million dollars on the PGA Tour before turning his attention to the Senior Tour in 1991.

QUIZ: What four events did Bobby Jones win when he captured the Grand Slam in 1930?

Chip Shot
A golf hole should be four inches deep.

QUIZ ANSWER: Jones won the U.S. Open, British Open, U.S. Amateur and the British Amateur.

JANUARY 15th

TODAY'S THOUGHT: "All men are created equal and I am one shot better than the rest." —Gene Sarazen

HISTORY: On this date in 1991 Beth Daniel was named the Associated Press' Female Athlete of the Year for 1990. Daniel was the LPGA Tour's leading money-winner for the year.

QUIZ: Name the only major won by Tom Weiskopf in his PGA career.

Chip Shot

When municipal course pro Jack Fleck beat Ben Hogan in a playoff to win the 1955 U.S. Open, he was using a set of Ben Hogan golf clubs.

QUIZ ANSWER: Weiskopf won the British Open in 1973.

JANUARY 16th

TODAY'S THOUGHT: "Golf is a way of testing ourselves while enjoying ourselves." —*Arnold Palmer*

HISTORY: On this date in 1994 Brett Ogle overtook Davis Love III to win the Hawaiian Open by one stroke. Ogle's birdie, coupled with Love's bogey, on the 17th hole gave the Australian his second victory in the United States.

QUIZ: What do Al Geiberger and Chip Beck have in common?

Chip Shot

Golfers have to be 50 years old to play in the U.S. Senior Open.

QUIZ ANSWER: Both have shot rounds of 59.

JANUARY 17th

TODAY'S THOUGHT: "Golf is the only sport where the object is to play as little as possible."
—*Charles G. McLoughlin, writer*

HISTORY: On this date in 1916 the Professional Golfers Association was established in New York City.

QUIZ: Four golfers have had 10 or more wins on the PGA Tour before reaching their 30th birthdays. Jack Nicklaus had 30 and Arnold Palmer had 10. Who are the other two?

Chip Shot
A survey by the National Golf Foundation revealed that the average, not pro, golfer averages a 97 for 18 holes.

QUIZ ANSWER: Johnny Miller had 17 wins and Tom Watson collected 16.

JANUARY 18th

TODAY'S THOUGHT: "Golf is a friend. A friend is an antidote for despair." —*Bob Toski*

HISTORY: On this date in 1992 Pat Bradley became the 12th player inducted into the LPGA Hall of Fame. Bradley had won her required 30th tournament during the previous season.

QUIZ: Sam Snead holds the record for most career wins on the PGA Tour. How many tournaments did Snead win?

Chip Shot
Pat Bradley once worked as a ski instructor before joining the LPGA Tour.

QUIZ ANSWER: Snead collected 84 wins in his career.

JANUARY 19th

TODAY'S THOUGHT: "If you think the game is just a matter of getting it close and letting the law of averages do your work for you, you'll find a different way to miss every time." —*Jack Nicklaus*

HISTORY: On this date in 1969 Miller Barber won the Kaiser International.

QUIZ: What course was the site of Arnold Palmer's only U.S. Open victory?

Chip Shot

The first time galleries were kept off the fairways and behind ropes at a tournament was in 1954 at the U.S. Open at Baltusrol Golf Club.

QUIZ ANSWER: Cherry Hills Country Club in Denver, Colorado

JANUARY 20th

TODAY'S THOUGHT: "Victory is everything. You can spend the money, but you can never spend the memories." —*Ken Venturi*

HISTORY: On this date in 1928 Lionel Hebert was born. Hebert made his mark in golf with a win in the 1957 PGA Championship.

QUIZ: Name the first golfer to win four U.S. Open titles.

Chip Shot

The record for playing in the most consecutive events on the PGA Tour without missing the cut is 113, held by Byron Nelson. Second is Jack Nicklaus with 105.

QUIZ ANSWER: Willie Anderson won the Open in 1901, '03, '04 and '05.

JANUARY 21st

TODAY'S THOUGHT: "We borrowed golf from Scotland as we borrowed whiskey. Not because it is Scottish, but because it is good."
—*Horace G. Hutchinson, golf historian*

HISTORY: On this date in 1940 Jack Nicklaus was born. Nicklaus is the golfer with the most major tournament wins in history.

QUIZ: 1988 was the first year that a player won more than a million dollars in one season on the PGA Tour. Who was it?

Chip Shot
Nicklaus made his debut on the PGA Tour at the 1962 Los Angeles Open...and finished last.

QUIZ ANSWER: Curtis Strange, with $1,147,644 that year

JANUARY 22nd

TODAY'S THOUGHT: "Golf is built around, and always will be built around, the amateur."
—*Phil Mickelson, 1990 U.S. Amateur champion*

HISTORY: On this date in 1995 Phil Mickelson became the first man to win the same tournament as an amateur and a professional when he captured the Northern Telecom Open.

QUIZ: Who holds the LPGA Tour record for consecutive victories?

Chip Shot
The 365 acres that house the Augusta National Golf Club were purchased by Bobby Jones and fellow investors for $70,000 in 1931.

QUIZ ANSWER: Nancy Lopez, with five in 1978

JANUARY 23rd

TODAY'S THOUGHT: "The harder you work, the luckier you get." —*Gary Player*

HISTORY: On this date in 1994 Andrew Magee ended a two-year victory drought with a win at the Northern Telecom Open.

QUIZ: These two University of Texas teammates finished tied for the individual collegiate championship in 1972. Who are they?

Chip Shot

The Walker Cup was donated in 1921 by George Herbert Walker, president of the USGA in 1920 and grandfather of President George Walker Bush.

QUIZ ANSWER: Ben Crenshaw and Tom Kite

JANUARY 24th

TODAY'S THOUGHT: "If you keep shooting par at them, they all crack sooner or later." —*Bobby Jones*

HISTORY: On this date in 1992 Mark Calcavecchia's 8-iron shot hit the flagstick on the 169-yard 4th hole and dropped in for an ace during the second round of the Phoenix Open.

QUIZ: What was Arnold Palmer's last win on the regular PGA Tour?

Chip Shot

Playing in the pro-am for the 1986 Chrysler Cup, Arnold Palmer holed-in-one on the third hole of the TPC at Avenel two days in a row.

QUIZ ANSWER: Palmer won the Bob Hope Desert Classic in 1973.

JANUARY 25th

TODAY'S THOUGHT: "Putting is the greatest psychological arena on the golf course, and many are the mighty who have fallen there."
—*Dr. David C. Morley*

HISTORY: On this date in 1964 PGA Tour player Billy Andrade was born. In 1991, Andrade was the only Tour player to win back-to-back tournaments.

QUIZ: True or false? The PGA Championship was once decided by match play.

Chip Shot

In 1962 Australian meteorologist Nils Lied hit a golf ball 2,640 yards across ice in Antarctica

---

QUIZ ANSWER: True. The 1958 championship was the first decided by stroke play.

JANUARY 26th

TODAY'S THOUGHT: "Golf is a negative sport, telling yourself over and over all the things that can go wrong, then not letting them." —*Tom Watson*

HISTORY: On this date in 1992 Bruce Lietzke scored a "freak of golf" when he followed an eagle on the third hole with an ace on the par-three fourth at the Phoenix Open. The back-to-back eagles didn't stop him from finishing nine strokes back of the leader.

QUIZ: What tournament did Jack Nicklaus win for his first victory as a pro?

Chip Shot

In 1953 Ben Hogan played in only six tournaments, winning five of them.

QUIZ ANSWER: The 1962 U.S. Open

JANUARY 27th

TODAY'S THOUGHT: "You don't hit anything with your backswing. So don't rush it." —*Doug Ford*

HISTORY: On this date in 1939 Mike Hill was born. An average player on the PGA Tour, Hill blossomed when he joined the Senior PGA Tour, winning five tournaments in both 1990 and '91.

QUIZ: Who was the first player to win a Senior PGA Tour event without ever winning on the regular tour?

Chip Shot

The first British Open was originally called a "General Golf Tournament for Scotland" and was "open" to only eight invited professionals. It was played at Prestwick in 1860.

QUIZ ANSWER: Walt Zembriski, who won the Newport Cup Tournament in 1988

JANUARY 28th

TODAY'S THOUGHT: "Golf is like art. It's impossible to be perfect." —*Sandra Palmer*

HISTORY: On this date in 1957 Nick Price was born. When Price won the British Open and PGA Championship in 1994, he became the first golfer in 70 years to win the two tournaments in the same year.

QUIZ: Who was the golfer who won both the British Open and PGA Championship in 1924?

Chip Shot

Gene Littler has the dubious distinction of playing in The Masters the most times without winning it. Littler entered 26 Masters between 1954 and 1980.

QUIZ ANSWER: Walter Hagen

JANUARY 29th

TODAY'S THOUGHT: "A club is like an automobile. Performance can make it look either ugly or beautiful." —*Gary Hallberg*

HISTORY: On this date in 1995 Raymond Floyd won the richest hole in skins history. Playing in the Senior Skins Game, Floyd birdied the 17th hole and walked away with $290,000.

QUIZ: What's my penalty if I'm closer to the hole than you are, but I hit first anyway?

Chip Shot
Research shows that, in a full drive by a male golfer, the clubhead swings through the ball at about 100 mph.

QUIZ ANSWER: There is no penalty. The ball shall be played where it lies.

JANUARY 30th

TODAY'S THOUGHT: "I don't have any big secret about putting. Just hit at it...it's either going to miss or go in." —*Ben Crenshaw*

HISTORY: On this date in 1955 Curtis Strange was born. Strange was the first golfer to win more than a million dollars in a year.

QUIZ: This golfer set the record when he shot a 257 over 72 holes at the 1955 Texas Open. Who was it?

Chip Shot
Local rule at the Jinja Golf Course in Uganda: If a ball comes to rest in dangerous proximity to a crocodile, another ball may be dropped.

QUIZ ANSWER: Mike Souchak

JANUARY 31st

TODAY'S THOUGHT: "The arc of your swing doesn't have a thing to do with the size of your heart."
—*Carol Mann*

HISTORY: On this date in 1993 63-year old Arnold Palmer successfully defended his title in the Senior Skins Game.

QUIZ: What golf course has the famous Road Hole as its seventeenth?

Chip Shot

Harry Vardon, J.H. Taylor and Gary Player are the only golfers to win the British Open in three different decades.

QUIZ ANSWER: The Old Course at St. Andrews in Scotland

FEBRUARY 1st

TODAY'S THOUGHT: "The hardest thing to learn about golf is keeping quiet about it."
—*George Houghton, writer*

HISTORY: On this date in 1968 W. Lawson Little died. Little was the 1940 U.S. Open winner and captured the U.S. and British Amateur titles in 1934 and '35.

QUIZ: This golfer won back-to-back British Opens in 1961 and '62. Who was it?

Chip Shot
In 1934 and '35, Little won 31 consecutive matches in the U.S. and British Amateur championships.

QUIZ ANSWER: Arnold Palmer

FEBRUARY 2nd

TODAY'S THOUGHT: "If you've got to remind yourself to concentrate during competition, you've got no chance to concentrate." —*Bobby Nichols*

HISTORY: On this date in 1949 Ben Hogan suffered near-fatal injuries when his car was hit head-on by a bus. Hogan recovered enough to be back on the tour in less than a year, winning the 1950 U.S. Open.

QUIZ: Where was the first Ryder Cup played in 1927?

Chip Shot
According to the USGA, if your driver is out of line by one degree, the ball will be off target by ten yards.

QUIZ ANSWER: The Worcester Country Club in Massachusetts

FEBRUARY 3rd

TODAY'S THOUGHT: "It's a compromise between what your ego wants you to do, what experience tells you to do, and what your nerves let you do."
—*Bruce Crampton, on tournament play*

HISTORY: On this date in 1941 Carol Mann was born. Mann was inducted into the LPGA Hall of Fame in 1977.

QUIZ: True or false? Jack Nicklaus and Tom Watson both attended Ohio State University.

Chip Shot
No American made it to the finals of the 1959 British Open.

QUIZ ANSWER: False. Nicklaus did attend Ohio State, but Watson went to school at Stanford.

FEBRUARY 4th

TODAY'S THOUGHT: "Make the hard ones look easy and the easy ones look hard." —*Walter Hagen*

HISTORY: On this date in 1979 JoAnne Carner bested Pat Bradley, 4 and 3, to take the Colgate Triple Crown at Mission Hills Country Club. Carner pocketed the first prize of $23,000.

QUIZ: Name the golfer who was nicknamed "Champagne Tony".

Chip Shot
The brothers Turnesa (Mike, Frank, Joe, Phil, Doug and Jim) all played professional golf in the '30's and '40's. A seventh brother, Willie, won the U.S. Amateur in 1938.

QUIZ ANSWER: Tony Lema

FEBRUARY 5th

TODAY'S THOUGHT: "Golf is one of the last refuges of real sport. You're your own policeman, and the behavior of its athletes is quite remarkable when you compare it to other sports." —*Jim McKay, announcer*

HISTORY: On this date in 1995 Peter Jacobsen ended a five-year victory drought with a win in the AT&T National Pro-Am in Pebble Beach.

QUIZ: What events make up the Women's Grand Slam?

Chip Shot

The youngest golfer to win the U.S. Open was Johnny McDermott, who was 19 when he won in 1911.

QUIZ ANSWER: The U.S. Women's Open, the LPGA Championship, the Nabisco Dinah Shore and the duMaurier Classic

FEBRUARY 6th

TODAY'S THOUGHT: "I don't know of any game that makes you so ashamed of your profanity. It is a game full of moments of self-abasement, with only a few moments of self-exaltation."
—*President William Howard Taft, on golf*

HISTORY: On this date in 1971 Alan Shepard took a mulligan on the moon but connected solidly with a 6-iron on his second shot.

QUIZ: True or false? Charley Seaver, a member of the 1932 U.S. Walker Cup team, is the father of former pitcher Tom Seaver.

Chip Shot

Shepard's swing was meant to test the moon's gravity.

QUIZ ANSWER: True

FEBRUARY 7th

TODAY'S THOUGHT: "Golf is a game played on a five-inch course between the ears." —*Bobby Jones*

HISTORY: On this date in 1993 Tammie Green beat Hall of Famer JoAnne Carner in a playoff to win the Palm Beach Classic championship.

QUIZ: Of all the players to ever win a major title, who comes first alphabetically?

Chip Shot
Between 1936 and 1979 Art Wall scored 43 holes-in-one, more than any other professional golfer.

QUIZ ANSWER: Tommy Aaron, who won the 1973 Masters

FEBRUARY 8th

TODAY'S THOUGHT: "How well you play golf depends on how well you control that left hand of yours." —*Tommy Armour*

HISTORY: On this date in 1987 Nancy Lopez qualified for the LPGA Hall of Fame by winning the Sarasota Classic, her 35th career victory.

QUIZ: If your driver breaks after hitting a ball during a match, are you allowed to replace it?

Chip Shot
The first win of Lopez' professional career came in 1978...at the Sarasota Classic.

QUIZ ANSWER: Yes, if you do not delay play. However, if you've broken it in a fit of anger, you can't replace it.

FEBRUARY 9th

TODAY'S THOUGHT: "To watch a first-class field drive off must convince everyone that a golf ball can be hit in many ways."

—*Henry Cotton, 1934 British Open champion*

HISTORY: On this date in 1992 the courageous Shelley Hamlin fired a final round of 66 to win the Phar-Mor at Inverrary. The victory, her first in 14 years, came seven months after she underwent a mastectomy.

QUIZ: Who is the only golfer to win six British Opens?

Chip Shot
Despite losing an eye in World War I, Tommy Armour still won three major titles.

QUIZ ANSWER: Harry Vardon

FEBRUARY 10th

TODAY'S THOUGHT: "The day you think you've got your swing down pat, something goes awry and you've got to go back to the driving range." —*Greg Norman*

HISTORY: On this date in 1955 Greg Norman was born.

QUIZ: Name the golfer who chipped in from 35 yards on the second sudden-death hole of the 1987 Masters to seize victory from Greg Norman.

Chip Shot
During a tournament week, a PGA Tour field will use approximately 2,500 practice balls a day.

QUIZ ANSWER: Larry Mize

FEBRUARY 11th

TODAY'S THOUGHT: "The difference between Hogan and Palmer was that with Hogan, when he reached a green, the people stood up and applauded. When Palmer got there, they all whooped and hollered."
—*Nick Faldo*

HISTORY: On this date in 1973 Arnold Palmer won his 60th, and final, PGA Tour title.

QUIZ: What golfer holds the record for most career Tour victories?

Chip Shot
The 1965 U.S. Open was the first to be played in a four-day format of 18 holes each day. Before that, golfers played 18 holes the first two days and a 36-hole final day.

QUIZ ANSWER: Kathy Whitworth, with 88

FEBRUARY 12th

TODAY'S THOUGHT: "Golf is a good walk spoiled."
—*Mark Twain*

HISTORY: On this date in 1995 Peter Jacobsen continued his torrid playing, winning consecutive tournaments for the first time in his 19-year pro career. Jacobsen won the Buick Invitational a week after finishing first at the National Pro-Am.

QUIZ: 1990 was the first year a Senior PGA Tour player earned more than the PGA Tour's leading money-winner. Who was it?

Chip Shot
Jacobsen spends his spare time as lead singer for his band, Jake Trout and the Flounders.

QUIZ ANSWER: Lee Trevino, who made $1,190,518

FEBRUARY 13th

TODAY'S THOUGHT: "I hate to watch tennis, where you have the McEnroes and Connors and the language they use. Golf is bigger than that." —*Tom Watson*

HISTORY: On this date in 1971 Vice-President Spiro Agnew teed off at the Bob Hope Desert Classic. His drive ricocheted off the arms of a man and his wife. After apologizing, Agnew tried again. And hit them again!

QUIZ: Who was our first golfing president?

Chip Shot
Presidents Truman, Ford, Bush and Clinton played golf right-handed but were natural lefties.

QUIZ ANSWER: William Howard Taft, who played golf once a week

FEBRUARY 14th

TODAY'S THOUGHT: "A great golf hole is one which puts a question mark into the player's mind when he arrives on the tee to play it."
—*Mackenzie Ross, golf course architect*

HISTORY: On this date in 1912 Byron Nelson was born. Nelson took the golf world by storm in 1945 when he won 18 tournaments, 11 in a row.

QUIZ: The 3-hole stretch from the 11th to 13th holes at Augusta National is known by what nickname?

Chip Shot
Nelson actually won 12 in a row, but the event wasn't counted since its purse fell below the PGA minimum of $3,000.

QUIZ ANSWER: Amen Corner

FEBRUARY 15th

TODAY'S THOUGHT: "It's a helluva lot easier to make money with an education than it is with a golf club." —*Jack Burke, Jr.*

HISTORY: On this date in 1987 Chi Chi Rodriguez won the PGA Seniors Championship. It proved to be a very good year for Rodriguez, winning seven titles in all.

QUIZ: What is Chi Chi Rodriguez' real name?

Chip Shot

Don January won the first Senior PGA Tour event in 1980 at the Atlantic City (NJ) Senior International.

QUIZ ANSWER: Juan Rodriguez

FEBRUARY 16th

TODAY'S THOUGHT: "If you try to fight the course, it will beat you." —*Lou Graham*

HISTORY: On this date in 1992 Craig Parry slipped by six-time champ Greg Norman to win the Australian Masters. Norman bogeyed the 15th, 16th and 17th holes after Parry had tied him for the lead.

QUIZ: Name the only American golfer to win the British Open five times.

Chip Shot

PGA golfer Jay Haas' uncle is 1986 Masters champion Bob Goalby.

QUIZ ANSWER: Tom Watson, who won it in 1975, '77, '80, '82 and '83

FEBRUARY 17th

 TODAY'S THOUGHT: "I hit a hook that went so far out of bounds I almost killed a horse in some stables a cab ride away from the first fairway."
—*Mike Souchak, on his first pro tournament*

HISTORY: On this date in 1955 a sizzling 27 on the back nine enabled Mike Souchak to shoot a first round of 60 in the Texas Open.

QUIZ: Three players have hit 8 straight birdies in a round. Two of them are Bob Goalby and Dewey Arnette. Who's the third?

Chip Shot

Willie Anderson beat Alex Smith in the first playoff in the U.S. Open. The year was 1901.

QUIZ ANSWER: Fuzzy Zoeller

FEBRUARY 18th

 TODAY'S THOUGHT: "Everyone gets wounded in a game of golf. The trick is not to bleed."
—*Peter Dobereiner, writer*

HISTORY: On this date in 1962 Louise Suggs picked up the final win of her career at the St. Petersburg Open. The LPGA co-founder and Hall-of-Famer finished with 50 career victories.

QUIZ: I never won a major title on the PGA Tour, yet I was the winner in three of the first six U.S. Senior Opens. Who am I?

Chip Shot

The Irish Golfing Union is the oldest such organization in the world. It was founded in 1891.

QUIZ ANSWER: Miller Barber

FEBRUARY 19th

TODAY'S THOUGHT: "Sometimes you'd like to just stand there in the middle of the green and scream as loud as you can. But we're the perfect gentlemen." —*Raymond Floyd*

HISTORY: On this date in 1995 Kenny Perry held on to win the Bob Hope Classic by one stroke over David Duval. Perry won despite shooting par from the seventh hole on at the Bermuda Dunes golf course.

QUIZ: This NJ course is continually ranked as one of the best in the world, but the course has never hosted a U.S. Open. Name it.

Chip Shot
Golf carts are prohibited in all PGA, LPGA and USGA events.

QUIZ ANSWER: Pine Valley Golf Club in Clementon

FEBRUARY 20th

TODAY'S THOUGHT: "Golf is neither a microcosm of nor a metaphor for life. It is a sport, a bloodless sport, if you don't count ulcers." —*Dick Schaap, writer*

HISTORY: On this date in 1994 Mike Hill successfully defended his title at the Senior PGA Tour's IntelliNet Challenge.

QUIZ: True or false? Former Colorado defensive back Hale Irwin played one year of professional football before joining the PGA Tour.

Chip Shot
1920's trick-shot artist Jack Redmond once asked the King of Samoa what his handicap was. "Six wives," said the King.

QUIZ ANSWER: False

FEBRUARY 21st

TODAY'S THOUGHT: "I don't care what anybody says. The first tournament is not the hardest one to win. It's always the second one." —*John Daly*

HISTORY: On this date in 1993 22-year old Phil Mickelson conducted a putting clinic over the back nine to pull away to a four-shot victory at the Buick Invitational, his first win as a pro.

QUIZ: In the nineteenth century, most golf shafts were made of what type of wood?

Chip Shot
Between 1923 and his retirement in 1930, Bobby Jones finished first or second in every U.S. Open except 1927.

QUIZ ANSWER: Hickory

FEBRUARY 22nd

TODAY'S THOUGHT: "If you're going to miss 'em, miss 'em quick."
—*George Duncan, British Open champ, on putting*

HISTORY: On this date in 1992 96 golfers were invited to play in that year's Masters. But for the first time in 17 years, Tom Kite did not qualify.

QUIZ: In the 1980's only one golfer won more than five PGA Tour events in a year. Who was it?

Chip Shot
The only time a golfer tells the truth is when he calls another golfer a liar.

QUIZ ANSWER: Tom Watson, who won six tournaments in 1980

FEBRUARY 23rd

TODAY'S THOUGHT: "If you're not prepared, somewhere in the quiz there are going to be some questions you can't answer." —*Charles Coody*

HISTORY: On this date in 1992 a 16-foot birdie on the final hole gave Steve Pate a one-stroke win at the Buick Invitational.

QUIZ: In what event were Lee Trevino, Bobby Nichols and Jerry Heard playing when they were struck by lightning?

Chip Shot

According to the National Hole-in-One Association, more than 31 thousand aces were scored in 1988. Of those, 27 were scored after the player's ball hit a tree.

QUIZ ANSWER: The 1975 Western Open

FEBRUARY 24th

TODAY'S THOUGHT: "If you watch a game, it's fun. If you play it, it's recreation. If you work at it, it's golf." —*Bob Hope*

HISTORY: On this date in 1990 Beth Daniel shot 6-under par to win the Hawaiian Ladies Open. It was the first of two straight victories for Daniel.

QUIZ: My final round of 63, including eight birdies in the first 13 holes, propelled me to victory in the 1973 U.S. Open. Who am I?

Chip Shot

In 1986 Wayne Grady was disqualified from both the Phoenix and LA Opens for hitting someone else's ball.

QUIZ ANSWER: Johnny Miller

FEBRUARY 25th

TODAY'S THOUGHT: "The object of a bunker or trap is not only to punish a physical mistake, to punish lack of control, but also to punish pride and egotism."
—*Charles Blair MacDonald, writer*

HISTORY: On this date in 1951 Babe Zaharias and George Bolesta won the Orlando, Florida 2-Ball tournament. The win give Zaharias three straight victories to start the LPGA season.

QUIZ: Who won four consecutive PGA Championships in the 20's?

Chip Shot

George Duncan overcame a 13-stroke deficit to win the 1920 British Open.

QUIZ ANSWER: Walter Hagen, from 1924-27

FEBRUARY 26th

TODAY'S THOUGHT: "No matter how hard I try, I just can't seem to break sixty-four." —*Jack Nicklaus*

HISTORY: On this date in 1978 Jack Nicklaus closed with five birdies to win the Inverrary Classic by one stroke.

QUIZ: Only one man has ever won a major tournament by birdieing five of the last six holes. Who was it?

Chip Shot

77-year old John Protti played a round of golf at the Vancouver Golf Club in 1994 after presenting a rain check dated April 7, 1948.

QUIZ ANSWER: Art Wall, in the 1959 Masters

FEBRUARY 27th

TODAY'S THOUGHT: "Bad golf is played with the shoulders and the body; good golf is played with the hands." —*Gene Sarazen*

HISTORY: On this date in 1901 Gene Sarazen was born. Sarazen was the first golfer to win each of the four modern Grand Slam championships.

QUIZ: Besides Gene Sarazen, three other golfers have won all four major championships. Who are they?

Chip Shot
Sarazen scored a hole-in-one in the 1973 British Open at the age of 71.

QUIZ ANSWER: Ben Hogan, Jack Nicklaus and Gary Player

FEBRUARY 28th

TODAY'S THOUGHT: "It is this constant and undying hope for improvement that makes golf so exquisitely worth the playing." —*Bernard Darwin, writer*

HISTORY: On this date in 1971 Jack Nicklaus won his second PGA Championship by two strokes over Billy Casper. The victory meant Nicklaus possessed a second set of the four major titles.

QUIZ: This golf course is the home of the Los Angeles Open. Name it.

Chip Shot
The tee at the first hole of the Homestead in Hot Springs, West Virginia has been in use since 1892.

QUIZ ANSWER: The Riviera Country Club

FEBRUARY 29th

TODAY'S THOUGHT: "Spring was designed like an old set of MacGregor irons — to rejuvenate the soul."
—*Deane Beman*

HISTORY: On this date in 1992 Dawn Coe won the Women's Kemper Open on the Wailea Golf Club Blue Course in Kihei, Maui, Hawaii. Her first win since joining the LPGA Tour in 1982, Coe earned $75,000.

QUIZ: What LPGA player is nicknamed "Big Mama"?

Chip Shot

According to the Guinness Book of Records, the longest drive on a standard course is 515 yards, by Michael Hoke Austin in 1974.

QUIZ ANSWER: JoAnne Carner

The Bathroom Golf Almanac

MARCH 1st

TODAY'S THOUGHT: "The cause of stress during a golf match, or anywhere else for that matter, is largely within yourself." —*Thomas N. Dorsel*

HISTORY: On this date in 1992 Fred Couples won the LA Open for the second time in three years. Couples rolled in a birdie putt on the second playoff hole to beat Davis Love III.

QUIZ: The USGA recommends that the flagstick be how high?

Chip Shot

Only two players have won the U.S. Open and U.S. Amateur in the same year. Chick Evans, Jr. did it in 1916 while Bobby Jones won both events in 1930.

QUIZ ANSWER: Seven feet

MARCH 2nd

TODAY'S THOUGHT: "Golf is a total obsession: the chess of sports, the only sport that requires total intelligence." —*James Woods, actor*

HISTORY: On this date in 1958 Ian Woosnam was born. The Welshman won the green jacket at The Masters in 1991 for his first major title.

QUIZ: If Tommy Aaron is first on the alphabetical list of players who have ever won a major, who's last?

Chip Shot

The most consecutive years a player has led the PGA Tour money list is four. Tom Watson was the biggest money winner between 1977 and 1980.

QUIZ ANSWER: Fuzzy Zoeller

MARCH 3rd

TODAY'S THOUGHT: "The place of the father in the modern suburban family is a very small one — particularly if he plays golf." *—Bertrand Russell*

HISTORY: On this date in 1920 Julius Boros was born. The PGA Hall-of-Famer won the U.S. Open in 1952 and 1963 and added a PGA Championship title to his belt at the age of 48 in 1968.

QUIZ: I never won The Masters. However, I did finish second four times in my career. Who am I?

Chip Shot

The first playoff between American players at the British Open was in 1933. Denny Shute beat Craig Wood.

QUIZ ANSWER: Tom Weiskopf

MARCH 4th

TODAY'S THOUGHT: "Golf is not a funeral, although both can be very sad affairs." *—Bernard Darwin, writer*

HISTORY: On this date in 1950 Judy Dickinson was born. During the 1985 U.S. Women's Open, Dickinson's round of 65 tied the record for the lowest round under par ever recorded in USGA history.

QUIZ: Can you name the first golfer to break 70 in all four rounds of a major championship?

Chip Shot

Greg Norman and Craig Wood share the dubious honor of having lost all four majors in playoffs.

QUIZ ANSWER: Arnold Palmer

MARCH 5th

TODAY'S THOUGHT: "Putting is three things: the line, the length and the stroke." —*Nick Faldo*

HISTORY: On this date in 1995 Nick Faldo won his first tournament on U.S. soil in almost five years. Faldo's victory at the Doral Ryder Open was his first since winning The Masters in 1990.

QUIZ: What's the modern-day name for the "niblick"?

Chip Shot

The only brothers to win the PGA Championship were Lionel (1957) and Jay (1960) Herbert.

QUIZ ANSWER: The 9-iron

MARCH 6th

TODAY'S THOUGHT: "A man's true colors will surface quicker in a five-dollar nassau than in any other form of diversion." —*Grantland Rice*

HISTORY: On this date in 1988 Orville Moody blistered the field at the Vintage International. Moody set a Senior PGA Tour record with a final round 63 to finish the tournament 25 shots under par.

QUIZ: Excluding the British Isles, where was the first golf course?

Chip Shot

The 1954 World Championship, won by Bob Toski, was golf's first $50,000 first prize.

QUIZ ANSWER: The Royal Calcutta Golf Club in India was established in 1829.

MARCH 7th

TODAY'S THOUGHT: "The guy who chokes least wins the most." —*Hubert Green*

HISTORY: On this date in 1993 Greg Norman set a tournament record on his way to victory at the Doral Open. Norman's 265 total broke the record set by Hubert Green by five strokes.

QUIZ: From 1960 to 1968 the Vardon Trophy for best scoring average was shared by what two players?

Chip Shot

The first British monarch to attend the British Open was King George VI. The king appeared at the 1948 Open.

QUIZ ANSWER: Billy Casper, who won the trophy 5 times, and Arnold Palmer who won it the other four years

MARCH 8th

TODAY'S THOUGHT: "A lot of times putting comes down to the guts of the putter — not being afraid to lose." —*Curtis Strange*

HISTORY: On this date in 1992 Raymond Floyd became the second man to win PGA Tour titles in four different decades with a two-stroke victory in the Doral Open. Sam Snead was the first.

QUIZ: True or false? Lee Trevino is one of a long line of golfers who attended the University of Texas.

Chip Shot

A golf cart is started and stopped an average of 150 times during a round of golf.

QUIZ ANSWER: False. Trevino never attended college.

MARCH 9th

TODAY'S THOUGHT: "I'm going to miss at least seven shots in every 18 holes, so if I'm going to be angry, I might as well start right on the first tee."
—*Walter Hagen*

HISTORY: On this date in 1941 Jim Colbert was born. Colbert won Rookie of the Year honors on the Senior PGA Tour when he won three tournaments in 1991.

QUIZ: In which movie does James Bond play golf against the villain?

Chip Shot

The 630-yard, par-5 17th hole at Baltusrol GC is the longest ever played in a men's major championship.

QUIZ ANSWER: "Goldfinger"

MARCH 10th

TODAY'S THOUGHT: "Relax? How can anybody relax and play golf? You have to grip the club, don't you?"
—*Ben Hogan*

HISTORY: On this date in 1991 35 mph gusts sent scores sailing at the Honda Classic. Steve Pate's 3-over-par 75 was enough to give him the win.

QUIZ: Name the golfer who's been the leading money winner on the PGA Tour the most times.

Chip Shot

In 1971 Lee Trevino captured three national titles over a 20-day period. Trevino won the U.S. Open, the Canadian Open and the British Open in succession.

QUIZ ANSWER: Jack Nicklaus, who led the way eight times

MARCH 11th

TODAY'S THOUGHT: "When one wants to play golf, one wants to be alone with nature."
—Alister MacKenzie, course designer

HISTORY: On this date in 1945 Byron Nelson began his record 11-event winning streak with a victory at the Miami Four Ball Tournament.

QUIZ: Two players with exactly three letters in their last name have won a major title. Name them.

Chip Shot

Nelson and Harold McSpaden became known as the "Gold Dust Twins" that year because the tournaments Nelson didn't win, McSpaden usually did.

QUIZ ANSWER: Edward Ray and Ernie Els

MARCH 12th

TODAY'S THOUGHT: "There's no better game in the world when you are in good company, and no worse game when you are in bad company." *—Tommy Bolt*

HISTORY: On this date in 1961 Mickey Wright defended her LPGA Championship crown with a nine-stroke win over Louise Suggs.

QUIZ: What male golfer was honored with a U.S. postage stamp in 1981?

Chip Shot

During World War II British golfers were asked to pick up bomb and shell fragments off the course to help the greenkeeper spare damage to the lawn mowers.

QUIZ ANSWER: Bobby Jones

MARCH 13th

 TODAY'S THOUGHT: "Golf is an easy game...it's just hard to play." —*Anonymous*

HISTORY: On this date in 1994 Nick Price captured the Honda Classic. But the spotlight was focused on John Daly, who was returning to the Tour after a suspension for quitting in the middle of a round the previous fall. Daly finished fourth, four strokes behind Price.

QUIZ: Can you name the only major title Sam Snead never won in his illustrious career?

Chip Shot

26-year old Nancy Lopez was the youngest player, male or female, to earn more than $1 million in her career.

QUIZ ANSWER: Snead never won the U.S. Open.

MARCH 14th

 TODAY'S THOUGHT: "It is easier to tell a man that there's something wrong with his wife and child than with his golf course." —*Frank Hannigan*

HISTORY: On this date in 1993 Meg Mallon edged Betsy King by one stroke to win the Ping-Welch's Championship. Mallon's tournament included three bogey-free rounds.

QUIZ: Legal or illegal? Just before putting, I use my club to flatten a few spike marks which are on my line.

Chip Shot

Bob Charles is the only left-handed golfer to ever win the British Open. The New Zealander did it in 1963.

QUIZ ANSWER: Illegal — It's a two-stroke penalty.

MARCH 15th

 TODAY'S THOUGHT: "Look like a woman, but play like a man." —*Jan Stephenson*

HISTORY: On this date in 1987 fortune smiled on Don Pooley. Pooley aced the 192-yard 17th hole at the Hertz Bay Classic and collected a half-million dollar bonus, the largest single-hole prize in golf history.

QUIZ: What was Babe Zaharias' real name?

Chip Shot
Kathy Whitworth and Mickey Wright combined for 170 victories on the LPGA Tour.

QUIZ ANSWER: Mildred Ella Zaharias got the nickname, Babe, when she hit five home runs as a kid.

MARCH 16th

 TODAY'S THOUGHT: "When I play my best golf, I feel as if I'm in a fog, standing back watching the earth in orbit with a golf club in your hands." —*Mickey Wright*

HISTORY: On this date in 1957 Patty Berg won her record-setting seventh Titleholders Championship.

QUIZ: Name the first foreigner to pass the million dollar mark in the LPGA.

Chip Shot
Sam Snead had to be persuaded by fellow pro, Johnny Bussa, to enter the 1946 British Open. Snead won, while Bulla finished tied for second.

QUIZ ANSWER: Australian Jan Stephenson, in 1985

MARCH 17th

TODAY'S THOUGHT: "It's a shame, but he'll never make a golfer. Too much temper."
—*Alex Smith, golf pro, on 13-year old Bobby Jones*

HISTORY: On this date in 1902 golfing legend Bobby Jones was born. Known as the best amateur player ever, Jones won 13 tournaments, including the Grand Slam, before retiring at age 28.

QUIZ: Quick! Which state has the most golf courses?

Chip Shot

The portrait of Bobby Jones that hangs in the Jones Cabin at Augusta National Golf Club was painted by Dwight D. Eisenhower.

QUIZ ANSWER: Florida, with California close behind

MARCH 18th

TODAY'S THOUGHT: "That little white ball won't move until you hit it, and there's nothing you can do after it has gone." —*Babe Zaharias*

HISTORY: On this date in 1951 amateur Pat Sullivan won the Titleholders Championship, stopping Babe Zaharias' consecutive victory streak at three.

QUIZ: In 1986 this golfer shot a final-round 63, but still finished second to Jack Nicklaus in The Masters. Who was it?

Chip Shot

The first time an LPGA Tour event was televised was in 1963. ABC carried the final round of the U.S. Women's Open from Cincinnati.

QUIZ ANSWER: Nick Price

MARCH 19th

 TODAY'S THOUGHT: "Fifty percent of the fairways we play on today are better than ninety percent of the greens we played on thirty years ago."
—Jim Ferree, Senior PGA Tour player

HISTORY: On this date in 1950 Babe Zaharias won her second U.S. Women's Open.

QUIZ: The oldest golf club in North America is located in what Canadian city?

Chip Shot

Golfers on the PGA Tour are not allowed to play more than one ball during a practice round.

QUIZ ANSWER: Montreal — The Royal Montreal Golf Club was founded in 1873.

MARCH 20th

 TODAY'S THOUGHT: "Golf is a typical capitalist lunacy of upperclass Edwardian England."
—George Bernard Shaw

HISTORY: On this date in 1937 golfing great Harry Vardon died. Vardon won the British Open a record six times, and was known for the grip that bears his name.

QUIZ: What's the oldest event on the PGA Tour?

Chip Shot

The U.S. Open was first televised in 1947; the British Open in 1955; and The Masters in 1956.

QUIZ ANSWER: The U.S. Open, which was first held in 1895

MARCH 21st

TODAY'S THOUGHT: "Golf is an indispensable adjunct to high civilization." —*Andrew Carnegie*

HISTORY: On this date in 1982 Jerry Pate won the Tournament Players Championship at the new, and difficult, TPC at Sawgrass. Pate celebrated by dragging commissioner Deane Beman, designer Pete Dye and himself into the lake next to the 18th green.

QUIZ: Two players have won the Vardon Trophy five times in their careers. One of them is Billy Casper. Who's the other golfer?

Chip Shot

Harvey Penick's "Little Red Book" is the best-selling sports book in history with more than one million copies sold.

QUIZ ANSWER: Lee Trevino

MARCH 22nd

TODAY'S THOUGHT: "I could make a pretty fair appraisal of the worth of an opponent simply by speaking to him on the first tee and taking a good measuring look into his eyes." —*Bobby Jones*

HISTORY: On this date in 1992 the race was for second place at the Nestle Invitational. Fred Couples led from start to finish to win by nine strokes.

QUIZ: Tom Watson's pitch from the rough on seventeen helped him win the 1982 U.S. Open. Name the course.

Chip Shot

One of Jack Nicklaus' victims on his march to the 1959 U.S. Amateur title was Robert T. Jones III, son of Bobby Jones.

QUIZ ANSWER: Pebble Beach Golf Links

MARCH 23rd

TODAY'S THOUGHT: "Hickory golf was a game of manipulation and inspiration; steel golf is a game of precision and calculation." —*Peter Dobereiner, writer*

HISTORY: On this date in 1980 Lee Trevino won the Tournament Players Championship. The event was one of three victories for Trevino that year.

QUIZ: In 1986 I led each major after three rounds, but only won one of the championships. Who am I?

Chip Shot
The Rules of Golf prevent a caddie from shielding a player from the elements while playing a stroke.

QUIZ ANSWER: Greg Norman, who won the British Open

MARCH 24th

TODAY'S THOUGHT: "They were real golfers, for real golf is a thing of the spirit, not of mere mechanical excellence of stroke." —*P.G. Wodehouse, "A Woman Is Only A Woman"*

HISTORY: On this date in 1974 Johnny Miller won his fourth tournament of the year, leading the field at the Heritage Classic.

QUIZ: If a Walker Cup match is tied, which team keeps the Cup?

Chip Shot
Teyateyaneng GC in South Africa has a par three of 67 yards. It also has a par five measuring 619 yards.

QUIZ ANSWER: In the event of a tie, the Cup is retained for another two years by the previous winner.

MARCH 25th

TODAY'S THOUGHT: "Good corn whiskey. It was a fun sort of tournament, that first one. They had 50 gallons and ran out by mid-morning of the third day of the tournament."

—*Paul Runyan, memories of the first Masters*

HISTORY: On this date in 1934 play concluded at the first Masters at Augusta National. Horton Smith held on to defeat Craig Wood by one stroke.

QUIZ: This golfer lost two Masters playoffs, one each to Byron Nelson and Sam Snead. Name him.

Chip Shot
Craig Wood finished second in the first two Masters.

QUIZ ANSWER: Ben Hogan

MARCH 26th

TODAY'S THOUGHT: "When our putting is sour, then we are in honest, interminable, miserable trouble."
—*Arnold Palmer*

HISTORY: On this date in 1961 Lou Kretlow aced the par-4, 427-yard 16th hole at Oklahoma City's Lake Hefner Golf Course. Kretlow's tremendous drive hit in front of the green and rolled up into the hole.

QUIZ: What is an "albatross"?

Chip Shot
Arnold Palmer and Jack Nicklaus won at least one tournament on the PGA Tour for 17 consecutive years, a record.

QUIZ ANSWER: "Albatross" is the British term for a double-eagle.

MARCH 27th

TODAY'S THOUGHT: "I never knew what top golf was like until I turned professional — then it was too late." —*Steve Melnyk*

HISTORY: On this date in 1994 Donna Andrews captured the first major title of her career, winning the Nabisco Dinah Shore.

QUIZ: What is the penalty in stroke play for carrying an extra club?

Chip Shot
In golf, nothing counts like your opponent.

QUIZ ANSWER: You're penalized two strokes for every hole, with a maximum penalty of four strokes. You're disqualified if you don't discard it after realizing the mistake.

MARCH 28th

TODAY'S THOUGHT: "In every tournament there are a few rounds of super golf; without a doubt they are played subconsciously." —*Chick Evans, Jr.*

HISTORY: On this date in 1993 Nick Price cruised to victory in the Players Championship at the TPC at Sawgrass. Price's 270 total was three strokes better than the course record set by Mark McCumber in 1988.

QUIZ: Who was the first golfer to win the U.S. Open and the U.S. Senior Open?

Chip Shot
The movie "Caddyshack" was filmed at the Rolling Hills Golf Resort in Ft. Lauderdale, Florida.

QUIZ ANSWER: Arnold Palmer

MARCH 29th

TODAY'S THOUGHT: "Golf is like a razor. You get just so sharp and then it begins to dull a little the more you use it." —*Doug Sanders*

HISTORY: On this date in 1992 Dottie Mochrie won the LPGA's first major tournament of the year. Mochrie stopped Julie Inkster's bid for a third Nabisco Dinah Shore title on the first hole of a playoff.

QUIZ: Quick! Who's known as "Super Mex"?

Chip Shot

A golfer cannot participate in any PGA Tour event until he's paid the $100 annual membership fee.

QUIZ ANSWER: Lee Trevino

MARCH 30th

TODAY'S THOUGHT: "The only thing that you should force in a golf swing is the club back into the bag." —*Byron Nelson*

HISTORY: On this date in 1889 after months of delay caused by the "Blizzard of '88", the first mixed foursome teed off at the St. Andrews Golf Club in Yonkers, NY.

QUIZ: Where is the Oakland Hills Country Club located?

Chip Shot

Seve Ballesteros was disqualified from the 1980 U.S. Open after a traffic tie-up caused Ballesteros to arrive late at the first tee.

QUIZ ANSWER: Birmingham, Michigan

MARCH 31st

 TODAY'S THOUGHT: "Competitors take bad breaks and use them to drive themselves just that much harder. Quitters take bad breaks and use them as reasons to give up." —*Nancy Lopez*

HISTORY: On this date in 1991 Amy Alcott won her record third Nabisco Dinah Shore Classic.

QUIZ: What female golfer was honored with a U.S. postage stamp in 1981?

Chip Shot
The first golf instruction book printed was "The Golfer's Manual", written by Henry B. Farnie in 1857.

QUIZ ANSWER: Babe Zaharias

APRIL 1st

TODAY'S THOUGHT: "Even the men's room has a double dogleg."
—*Dave Stockton, on the Poppy Hills Golf Course*

HISTORY: On this date in 1957 Donnie Hammond was born. Hammond made a run at the '92 British Open title before a 74 dropped him to fifth.

QUIZ: Can you name the Australian golfer who won three consecutive British Opens during the 1950's?

Chip Shot

Rocky Thompson won two Senior PGA Tour events in 1991. But on the PGA Tour, Thompson endured 28 years and 600 events without a victory.

QUIZ ANSWER: Peter Thomson, in 1952, '53 and '54

APRIL 2nd

TODAY'S THOUGHT: "It's number one for me, pure and simple, because it's golf. The other events have become tented villages and circuses. When you go the The Masters, the focus is golf." —*Greg Norman*

HISTORY: On this date in 1939 Ralph Guldahl, coming off back-to-back wins in the U.S. Open, won The Masters.

QUIZ: Who was the first African-American golfer in The Masters?

Chip Shot

If you're an average 150-pound male who walks the course and pulls golf clubs while playing 18 holes, expect to burn about 1,060 calories.

QUIZ ANSWER: Lee Elder, in 1975

APRIL 3rd

TODAY'S THOUGHT: "If the putts go in, it's your week. If they don't go in, it's not your week. It's that simple." —*Ian Woosnam*

HISTORY: On this date in 1992 Chip Beck set a two-round tournament record at the $1 million Freeport McMoRan Golf Classic. Beck's 36-hole total of 132 broke the 1989 record by one stroke.

QUIZ: What LPGA golfer won The Vare Trophy, for lowest scoring average, a record seven times in her career?

Chip Shot

Built in 1895, the Van Cortlandt Park Golf Course in the Bronx (NY) was the first public golf course in the U.S.

QUIZ ANSWER: Kathy Whitworth

APRIL 4th

TODAY'S THOUGHT: "The job of a finishing hole is as clearly defined as that of a dance hall bouncer. It has to maintain order, clear out the amateurs, preserve the dignity of the game." —*Jim Murray, writer*

HISTORY: On this date in 1937 Byron Nelson won the first of his two Masters titles.

QUIZ: True or false? Arnold Palmer and Curtis Strange attended the same university.

Chip Shot

During World War II only four major championships were played: the '42 Masters and the '42, '44 and '45 PGA Championships.

QUIZ ANSWER: True. Both went to Wake Forest University.

APRIL 5th

TODAY'S THOUGHT: "It's nice to have the opportunity to play for so much money, but it's nicer to win it."
—*Patty Sheehan*

HISTORY: On this date in 1959 Art Wall came from six strokes down, firing a 66 in the final round at Augusta to win The Masters.

QUIZ: Name the only two South African golfers to win the U.S. Open.

Chip Shot

Masters champions do not use the same locker room as the rest of the competitors. They have their own facility which is off-limits to everyone else.

QUIZ ANSWER: Gary Player, who won his title in 1965, and Ernie Els, who won the championship in 1994

APRIL 6th

TODAY'S THOUGHT: "There are two kinds of golf — golf and tournament golf. The latter is an aging game."
—*Bobby Jones*

HISTORY: On this date in 1936 Horton Smith battled a wet Augusta National golf course to win his second Masters tournament in three years.

QUIZ: Before the invention of wooden tees, what did golfers use?

Chip Shot

In 1888 the St. Andrew's GC of Yonkers, NY spent a total of $28.42 for the upkeep of the six-hole golf course.

QUIZ ANSWER: Sand—A sandbox was located near the tee area from which the golfer or his caddy would grab a pinch of wet sand.

APRIL 7th

TODAY'S THOUGHT: "Nicklaus will never be a hungry golfer as Palmer and Player and Sanders and Snead and Hogan and all the other successful ones have been in their time." —*"Sports Illustrated", 1962*

HISTORY: On this date in 1963 23-year old Jack Nicklaus became the youngest golfer to wear the green jacket when he edged Tony Lema by one stroke to win The Masters.

QUIZ: What golfing great was nicknamed "The Hawk"?

Chip Shot

Sam Snead's PGA Tour victories span a record 29 years, from his first win in 1936 to his last in 1965.

QUIZ ANSWER: Ben Hogan

APRIL 8th

TODAY'S THOUGHT: "Golf is really two games. One is the game in the air. The golfer can lick that part of the game." —*Claude Harmon*

HISTORY: On this date in 1990 Nick Faldo defeated Raymond Floyd in a playoff to become the second player to defend his Masters title. Jack Nicklaus had won back-to-back titles in 1965 and '66.

QUIZ: The first defeat on home soil for the United States Ryder Cup team occurred at the Muirfield GC. What was the year?

Chip Shot

The Masters was the first major to switch from an 18-hole playoff to sudden death, making the change in 1976.

QUIZ ANSWER: 1987

APRIL 9th

TODAY'S THOUGHT: "Putting is simple. You need a sound putting stroke, confidence, patience, feel and visualization." —*Seve Ballesteros*

HISTORY: On this date in 1978 Gary Player rose to the challenge at The Masters. Trailing by seven strokes on the final day, Player shot a record-tying 64 to win his third green jacket at Augusta.

QUIZ: Only one golfer won two Masters titles in the 1980's. Who?

Chip Shot

The Puntas Arenas GC in Chile is the southernmost course in the world. Because of strong winds, the greens are set below the fairway level.

QUIZ ANSWER: Seve Ballesteros, in 1980 and '83

APRIL 10th

TODAY'S THOUGHT: "You never get golf. You play well one day, at least you play well for you, and you think you've got it. But you go out the next day and you haven't got it. Instead, it's got you."
—*John Madden, announcer*

HISTORY: On this date in 1916 Englishman Jim Barnes won the first PGA Championship at the Siwanoy Golf Course in Bronxville, NY.

QUIZ: Who won the first U.S. Senior Open?

Chip Shot

Walter Hagen reached the finals of the PGA Championship five straight times when the event was played at match play. He also had four consecutive victories.

QUIZ ANSWER: Roberto deVicenzo

APRIL 11th

TODAY'S THOUGHT: "He's the best there ever was in the game, and if a man doesn't want to play the best, he doesn't like ice cream."
—*Lee Trevino, on competing with Nicklaus*

HISTORY: On this date in 1966 Jack Nicklaus successfully defended his Masters title with a playoff win over Tommy Jacobs and Gay Brewer.

QUIZ: Legal or illegal? I ask you what club you just hit.

Chip Shot
The first recorded hole-in-one is credited to Young Tom Morris in the 1868 British Open.

QUIZ ANSWER: Illegal. It's a two-stroke penalty for me, but, if you answer me you also get a two-stroke penalty.

APRIL 12th

TODAY'S THOUGHT: "Arnold Palmer is the king of kings. Anybody who resents Arnold getting more attention than the rest of us doesn't deserve to use his head for more than a hat rack." —*Doug Sanders*

HISTORY: On this date in 1964 Arnold Palmer became the first golfer to win The Masters four times.

QUIZ: Name the president who was a member of the Augusta National Golf Club.

Chip Shot
Arnold Palmer broke 70 on the golf course before he hit the age of 12.

QUIZ ANSWER: Dwight D. Eisenhower

APRIL 13th

TODAY'S THOUGHT: "You can be the greatest iron player in the world or the greatest putter, but if you can't get the ball in position to use your greatness, you can't win." —*Ben Hogan*

HISTORY: On this date in 1997 Tiger Woods became the youngest golfer to win The Masters.

QUIZ: How many dimples are on the modern golf ball?

Chip Shot

The course at Augusta National GC was designed by Alister MacKenzie and Bobby Jones.

QUIZ ANSWER: 400

APRIL 14th

TODAY'S THOUGHT: "I am a stupid."
—*Roberto DeVicenzo, after the '68 Masters*

HISTORY: On this date in 1968 the last day of The Masters was not a happy birthday for Roberto DeVicenzo. His signing of an incorrect scorecard gave the title to Bob Goalby.

QUIZ: Name the first president of the Augusta National GC.

Chip Shot

Tommy Aaron, DeVicenzo's playing partner, put down a four on the Argentine's card instead of a three on the 71st hole.

QUIZ ANSWER: Bobby Jones

APRIL 15th

TODAY'S THOUGHT: "The biggest liar in the world is the golfer who claims he plays the game merely for the exercise." —*Tommy Bolt*

HISTORY: On this date in 1979 Fuzzy Zoeller survived a playoff to become the first player to win The Masters in his initial appearance.

QUIZ: When I won The Masters in 1971, little did I know that would be the only major tournament win of my career. Who am I?

Chip Shot
Zoeller is the only golfer to win playoffs in majors under two formats, in sudden death and at the 1984 U.S. Open, beating Greg Norman over 18 holes.

QUIZ ANSWER: Charles Coody

APRIL 16th

TODAY'S THOUGHT: "Watching golf on TV is one thing. Trying to watch a golf tournament in person is like trying to cover a war on foot." —*Jay Cronley, writer*

HISTORY: On this date in 1958 Arnold Palmer won the first of his eight major championships with a one-stroke victory in The Masters.

QUIZ: Three golfers have won The Masters exactly three times. Two of them are Sam Snead and Gary Player. Who's the third?

Chip Shot
President Grover Cleveland decided against taking up golf in retirement, saying he was too fat.

QUIZ ANSWER: Jimmy Demaret

APRIL 17th

TODAY'S THOUGHT: "There's no such thing as a bad course. Courses are like people — each course has its own personality. You have to challenge each one as it comes along." —*Barbara Mizrahie*

HISTORY: On this date in 1994 Raymond Floyd hit three balls into the water on the final four holes, virtually handing Lee Trevino the PGA Seniors Championship. Trevino won by a stroke.

QUIZ: Where is the Inverness Club located?

Chip Shot
Eldrick "Tiger" Woods was the first golfer to repeat as U.S. Junior Amateur champion.

QUIZ ANSWER: Toledo, Ohio

APRIL 18th

TODAY'S THOUGHT: "It's all right to put all your eggs in one basket — if you've got the right basket." —*Sam Snead*

HISTORY: On this date in 1993 former steel worker Tom Wargo came out of nowhere to win the PGA Seniors Championship on the second hole of sudden death. Wargo defeated Bruce Crampton for the victory.

QUIZ: What's the modern-day name for the "mashie"?

Chip Shot
Wargo, who taught himself how to play golf, didn't take up the game until he was 25 years old.

QUIZ ANSWER: The 5-iron

APRIL 19th

TODAY'S THOUGHT: "There's no pressure. Mediocrity knows no pressure." —*Gary McCord*

HISTORY: On this date in 1992 Davis Love III became the first golfer to win the Heritage Classic three times.

QUIZ: Name one of the four players who aced the sixth hole in the same round of the 1989 U.S. Open at Oak Hill.

Chip Shot

The 9th hole at St. Andrews Old Course is named Bobby Jones. The 18th hole is named Old Tom Morris.

QUIZ ANSWER: Jerry Pate, Nick Price, Doug Weaver and Mark Wiebe each used a 7-iron on the 167-yard, par-3 hole.

APRIL 20th

TODAY'S THOUGHT: "There is nothing that will get your mind off everything like golf will. They say you can get so sore at yourself that you forget you hate your enemies." —*Will Rogers*

HISTORY: On this date in 1958 Louise Suggs shot three-under par for her second win in the Babe Zaharias Open.

QUIZ: You're on the first tee, ready to make your first shot of the day. What's the ruling if you accidentally knock the ball off the tee?

Chip Shot

Babe Zaharias was voted Woman Athlete of the First Half of the 20th Century in an Associated Press poll.

QUIZ ANSWER: No stroke, so no penalty

APRIL 21st

TODAY'S THOUGHT: "Golfers used to check the grass on the greens; today they study the roots under the blade." —*Jimmy Demaret*

HISTORY: On this date in 1991 Jack Nicklaus continued his hot start on the Senior PGA Tour. Winning the PGA Seniors Championship gave Nicklaus his fourth victory in six starts in his initial season.

QUIZ: What 1970 NFL MVP now plays on the Senior PGA Tour?

Chip Shot

Brandie Burton reached $1 million in career earnings in her third year on the LPGA Tour. Mickey Wright earned about $368,000 in her career — and she won 82 events!

QUIZ ANSWER: Former 49ers QB John Brodie

APRIL 22nd

TODAY'S THOUGHT: "I really don't like playoffs. I feel sorry for the other guy if I win and I feel worse if I lose." —*Chi Chi Rodriguez*

HISTORY: On this date in 1979 Tom Watson rebounded from a playoff loss in The Masters to win the Tournament of Champions.

QUIZ: Name the only golfer to win back-to-back British Opens in the 1970's.

Chip Shot

The 19th hole at Royal Troon, Scotland is called the "dirty bar" because players are permitted to drink in their golf attire rather than in jacket and tie.

QUIZ ANSWER: Lee Trevino, in 1971 and '72

APRIL 23rd

TODAY'S THOUGHT: "I like golf becauses when somebody tells the gallery to be quiet, they get quiet. Try that in baseball and they get louder."
—*Mark McGwire, baseball player*

HISTORY: On this date in 1944 Marty Fleckman was born. In 1967 Fleckman won the Cajun Classic, his first professional tournament.

QUIZ: What is the diameter of a golf ball?

Chip Shot
Former PGA Tour Commissioner and one-time Tour player Deane Beman is the only man to become commissioner of the major sport he played.

QUIZ ANSWER: 1.68 inches

APRIL 24th

TODAY'S THOUGHT: "I never saw a good player from the trees." —*Byron Nelson*

HISTORY: On this date in 1994 Mike Springer won for the first time on the PGA Tour, taking the Greater Greensboro Open by three strokes.

QUIZ: From 1949 to 1972 colleges from this state won 19 of the 24 NCAA Golf Championships. Name it.

Chip Shot
Jack Burke, Jr. won four straight events in 1952, the last golfer to win more than three in a row.

QUIZ ANSWER: Texas — Titles were won by Houston, North Texas States, SMU and Texas.

APRIL 25th

TODAY'S THOUGHT: "Gentlemen play golf. And if you aren't a gentleman when you start, after the crushing events of the game, you surely become one."
—*Bing Crosby*

HISTORY: On this date in 1993 it took four playoff holes before a winner emerged at the Greater Greensboro Open. Rocco Mediate came from four strokes down to edge Steve Elkington.

QUIZ: When was the last time an amateur won the U.S. Open?

Chip Shot
The first British Open played in England was in 1894. John H. Taylor won the silver jug at Royal St. George's.

QUIZ ANSWER: John Goodman won it in 1933.

APRIL 26th

TODAY'S THOUGHT: "The game was easy for me as a kid, and I had to play a while to find out how hard it is." —*Raymond Floyd*

HISTORY: On this date in 1992 Lee Trevino and Mike Hill held off all challengers to win the Legends of Golf.

QUIZ: In 1969 this golfer won the U.S. Women's Amateur, two years after walking away with the U.S. Women's Open title. Who was it?

Chip Shot
The 18th hole at Barton Creek Club in Austin, Texas has a natural cave located just short of the green.

QUIZ ANSWER: Catherine Lacoste

APRIL 27th

TODAY'S THOUGHT: "Golf is 90 percent inspiration, and 10 percent perspiration." —*Johnny Miller*

HISTORY: On this date in 1992 68-year old Joe Graney, who hit a hole-in-one only six days after a cataract was removed from his right eye, did it again. Graney knocked down an ace six days after cataract surgery on his left eye!

QUIZ: True or false? Nathanial Crosby, son of singer Bing Crosby, once won the U.S. Amateur.

Chip Shot
The first water hazards were streams running across Scottish links on their way to the sea.

QUIZ ANSWER: True. Crosby won in 1981.

APRIL 28th

TODAY'S THOUGHT: "You start to choke when you drive through the front gate. On the first hole, you just want to make contact with the ball." —*Hale Irwin*

HISTORY: On this date in 1966 John Daly was born. Daly burst onto the golf scene in fairy-tale fashion with a win in the 1991 PGA Championship.

QUIZ: Name the one major title Ben Crenshaw has won twice.

Chip Shot
The record for the longest putt holed in a major belongs to Nick Faldo. Faldo dropped in a 100-foot birdie on the second hole of the 1989 Masters.

QUIZ ANSWER: The Masters, in 1984 and 1995

APRIL 29th

TODAY'S THOUGHT: "I say this without any reservations whatsoever. It is impossible to outplay an opponent you can't out-think." —*Lawson Little*

HISTORY: On this date in 1927 Glenna Collett Vare turned down a $50,000 contract to play golf professionally, saying she only wanted to play golf for the love of the game.

QUIZ: What golfer set a record for the lowest stroke total ever in an American major at the 1994 PGA Championship?

Chip Shot

Vare won a record six U.S. Women's Amateur championships between 1922 and 1935. Call it "love".

QUIZ ANSWER: Nick Price, with an 11-under par 269

APRIL 30th

TODAY'S THOUGHT: "The putter is a club designed to hit the ball partway to the hole."
—*Rex Lardner, humorist*

HISTORY: On this date in 1972 Kathy Whitworth rang up another victory on the LPGA Tour. Whitworth shot ten-under par at the Alamo Ladies Open.

QUIZ: Kathy Whitworth won 88 tournaments in her career, but cannot count this major championship among them. Which one?

Chip Shot

What do you do when your playing partner claims to have found his ball in the rough, but you know he's lying because his ball is in your pocket?

QUIZ ANSWER: The U.S. Women's Open

MAY 1st

TODAY'S THOUGHT: "When it's going good, you love your putter. When it's going bad, it's like it has betrayed you and you want to throw the sucker into a lake." —*Ken Green*

HISTORY: On this date in 1994 the Houston Open produced a first-time winner on the PGA Tour for the fifth straight year. Rookie Mike Heinen took his turn, edging Hal Sutton by three strokes.

QUIZ: What is the diameter of a golf hole?

Chip Shot
Calvin Peete led the PGA Tour in driving accuracy ten straight years, 1981-90.

QUIZ ANSWER: 4.25 inches

MAY 2nd

TODAY'S THOUGHT: "Baseball player, football player, hockey player retires, he takes up golf. I've never heard of a golfer retiring and taking up hockey. This is the greatest game." —*Lee Trevino*

HISTORY: On this date in 1976 JoAnne Carner finished ten-under-par to win the Lady Tara Classic.

QUIZ: Who was the first South African golfer to win the British Open?

Chip Shot
Senior PGA Tour player Orville Moody is nicknamed "Sarge" because of the 14 years he spent in the Army.

QUIZ ANSWER: Bobby Locke, who won the championship in 1949, also won the Open in 1950, '52 and '57.

MAY 3rd

TODAY'S THOUGHT: "Golf is temporary insanity practiced in a pasture." —*Dave Kindred, writer*

HISTORY: On this date in 1987 Paul Azinger took home the richest prize in PGA Tour history when he won the Panasonic Las Vegas tournament. Azinger pocketed $250,000 with the triumph.

QUIZ: This famous seaside course with its feared 107-yard, par-3 7th hole was designed by amateur golfer Jack Neville in 1919. Name it.

Chip Shot
During that same tournament, Scott Hoch won a $118,000 Rolls Royce when he aced the 17th hole.

QUIZ ANSWER: Pebble Beach Golf Links in California

MAY 4th

TODAY'S THOUGHT: "Give me golf clubs, fresh air, and a beautiful partner...and she better be able to putt." —*Anonymous*

HISTORY: On this date in 1928 LPGA Hall of Famer Betsy Rawls was born. Rawls owns 55 LPGA victories, including eight major championships.

QUIZ: During the 1960's what two golfers from the PGA Tour were honored by "Sports Illustrated" as Sportsman of the Year?

Chip Shot
Rawls graduated Phi Beta Kappa from the University of Texas with a degree in mathematics and physics.

QUIZ ANSWER: Arnold Palmer won the award in 1960 and Ken Venturi was honored in 1964.

MAY 5th

TODAY'S THOUGHT: "If you have a bad grip, you don't want a good swing." —*Harvey Penick*

HISTORY: On this date in 1991 instant-replay was used for the first time in a tournament. Tom Kite lost a stroke when videotape showed that a tee shot into the water should have been replayed from the tee.

QUIZ: In 1933 I lost the British Open in a playoff. In 1935 I lost The Masters in a playoff. In 1939 I lost the U.S. Open in, yes, a playoff. Who am I?

Chip Shot

The practice range at Muirfield Village in Dublin, Ohio is circular so golfers can practice with the wind of their choice.

QUIZ ANSWER: Craig Wood

MAY 6th

TODAY'S THOUGHT: "I play this game because my sole ambition is to do well enough to give it up." —*David Feherty, on professional golf*

HISTORY: On this date in 1979 Nancy Lopez, on her way to Vare Trophy honors, won the Women's International. The tournament was one of eight victories for Lopez that year.

QUIZ: Name the native country of Ian Baker-Finch.

Chip Shot

A tap-in for par on the final hole of the 1970 British Open would have clinched the championship for Doug Sanders. He missed, and lost in a playoff the next day to Jack Nicklaus.

QUIZ ANSWER: Baker-Finch was born in Australia.

MAY 7th

TODAY'S THOUGHT: "It's good sportsmanship to not pick up lost golf balls while they are still rolling." —*Mark Twain*

HISTORY: On this date in 1995 Michelle McGann ended a seven-year victory drought, edging Laura Davies by one stroke at the Sara Lee Classic. McGann had earned over one million dollars in seven years on the LPGA Tour without a win.

QUIZ: Who's the oldest man to win the PGA Championship?

Chip Shot
Playing golf on Sunday instead of attending church was a crime in 16th century Scotland. The fine? 40 shillings.

QUIZ ANSWER: Julius Boros, 48 years old in 1968

MAY 8th

TODAY'S THOUGHT: "I owe everything to golf. Where else could a guy with an IQ like mine make this much money?" —*Hubert Green*

HISTORY: On this date in 1994 it took a four-foot birdie putt on the final hole to assure victory for John Daly in the BellSouth Classic. It was Daly's first win since the 1992 B.C. Open.

QUIZ: Who was the first player to win a million dollars while playing on the Senior PGA Tour?

Chip Shot
Golf's oldest trophy belongs to The Honourable Company of Edinburgh Golfers. It was first awarded in 1744.

QUIZ ANSWER: Don January crossed that threshold in 1985.

MAY 9th

TODAY'S THOUGHT: "There are many ways of performing the operation successfully. I can claim, however, to be in a position to explain how not to putt. I think I know as well as anybody how not to do it."
—*Harry Vardon*

HISTORY: On this date in 1870 Harry Vardon was born in Great Britain. Vardon won six British Opens and one U.S. Open.

QUIZ: Explain match vs. medal play.

Chip Shot
Nothing increases your golf score like witnesses.

QUIZ ANSWER: The winner at match play is determined by the total holes won while medal play is by total strokes.

MAY 10th

TODAY'S THOUGHT: "Golf and sex are about the only things you can enjoy without being good at it."
—*Jimmy Demaret*

HISTORY: On this date in 1910 the man who introduced sartorial splendor to the PGA Tour, Jimmy Demaret, was born. The Hall of Famer was also the first golfer to win three Masters championships.

QUIZ: Arnold Palmer lost three playoffs at the U.S. Open. To whom?

Chip Shot
In 1954 Demaret said he owned 71 pairs of slacks, 55 shirts, 39 sportcoats, 20 sweaters and 43 hats.

QUIZ ANSWER: Jack Nicklaus in 1962; Julius Boros in 1963; and Billy Casper in 1966

MAY 11th

TODAY'S THOUGHT: "If I ever needed an eight-foot putt and everything I owned depended on it, I would want Arnold Palmer to putt it for me." —*Bobby Jones*

HISTORY: On this date in 1959 Arnold Palmer finished 15-under-par to win the Oklahoma City Open, the 12th victory of his professional career.

QUIZ: What is the most common 18-hole par on golf courses?

Chip Shot

Americans won all but one British Open between 1921 and 1933. Briton Arthur Havers won it in 1923.

QUIZ ANSWER: 72

MAY 12th

TODAY'S THOUGHT: "Don't let the bad shots get to you. Don't let yourself become angry. The true scramblers are thick-skinned. And they always beat the whiners." —*Paul Runyan*

HISTORY: On this date in 1985 Kathy Whitworth won the United Virginia Bank Classic. The title was her 88th, and final, victory of her career.

QUIZ: Legal or illegal? In a bunker, I touch the sand with my club to determine its condition.

Chip Shot

The difference between learning to play golf and learning to drive a car is that, in golf, you never hit anything.

QUIZ ANSWER: Illegal—I am assessed a two-stroke penalty.

MAY 13th

TODAY'S THOUGHT: "I realize that's why we play golf, to hit the ball into the hole. But it's such a strange feeling when you hit an iron shot and it actually goes in." —*Hollis Stacy*

HISTORY: On this date in 1952 Mickey Wright passed Babe Zaharias on the alltime victory list, notching number 32 at the Western Open.

QUIZ: Five amateurs have won the U.S. Open, none since 1933. How many can you name?

Chip Shot
The first known women's tournament took place in Scotland in 1810. First prize was a fish basket.

QUIZ ANSWER: Francis Ouimet, Jerry Travers, Chick Evans, Bobby Jones and John Goodman

MAY 14th

TODAY'S THOUGHT: "The one stroke marks the difference between fame and oblivion."
—*Samuel L. Parrish, USGA official*

HISTORY: On this date in 1978 Nancy Lopez began her record-setting streak by capturing the Greater Baltimore Classic. Lopez went on to win five straight tournaments that she entered.

QUIZ: The first twelve British Opens were contested at this course in Scotland. Name it.

Chip Shot
Robert Trent Jones is given credit as the first golf course architect to use water hazards in his course designs.

QUIZ ANSWER: Prestwick Golf Club

MAY 15th

TODAY'S THOUGHT: "Golf was never meant to be an exact science; it's an art form. Einstein was a great scientist but a lousy golfer." —*Bob Toski*

HISTORY: On this date in 1991 the LPGA announced an anti-discrimination policy, saying that as of the following year, tournaments would no longer be held at golf clubs that excluded minorities.

QUIZ: What Hall of Famer has won the most majors on the LPGA Tour?

Chip Shot

The worst loss in playoff history was suffered by Al Espinosa, who finished 23 strokes behind Bobby Jones over 36 holes in the 1929 U.S. Open.

QUIZ ANSWER: Patty Berg, with 16

MAY 16th

TODAY'S THOUGHT: "In football, some coaches have stated, when you throw a pass, three things can happen, two of them are bad. In golf, there is no limit." —*Mario Parascenzo, writer*

HISTORY: On this date in 1993 Scott Simpson saved par on the final hole for a one-stroke victory in the Byron Nelson Classic.

QUIZ: This Texan won the 1965 PGA Championship. In 1981 he captained the U.S. to a Ryder Cup victory. Who is he?

Chip Shot

PGA Tour pro Billy Andrade was named all-state in basketball at Providence (RI) Country Day School.

QUIZ ANSWER: Dave Marr

MAY 17th

TODAY'S THOUGHT: "There is nothing like winning the Ryder Cup. It beats everything else because you are playing for someone else besides yourself and it means more." —*Tom Watson*

HISTORY: On this date in 1992 Betsy King laid claim to her first LPGA Championship.

QUIZ: If you cut a golf ball with your stroke, are you allowed to immediately replace it?

Chip Shot

Railroad president Walter Ross first proposed matches between the U.S. and Great Britain. But he didn't want to spend the money for a trophy. English merchant Samuel Ryder did.

QUIZ ANSWER: Yes.

MAY 18th

TODAY'S THOUGHT: "I don't have any big secret about putting. Just hit at it. It's either going to miss or go in." —*Ben Crenshaw*

HISTORY: On this date in 1986 Pat Bradley didn't win the Chrysler-Plymouth Classic, but her earnings did push her over the $2 million mark in her career, the first woman golfer to do so.

QUIZ: Only one golfer won the U.S. Open twice during the 70's. Who?

Chip Shot

Visitors aren't allowed to play the championship course at Royal Melbourne GC, host of every major Australian championship.

QUIZ ANSWER: Hale Irwin, in 1974 and '79

MAY 19th

TODAY'S THOUGHT: "Golf is a young man's vice and an old man's penance." —*Irving Cobb, humorist*

HISTORY: On this date in 1991 Kenny Perry thwarted Hale Irwin's comeback bid with a birdie on the first playoff hole to win the Memorial. Irwin had made up five shots over the final round to force sudden death.

QUIZ: The U.S. Open, first held in 1895, is the oldest tournament on the PGA Tour. What event is the second oldest?

Chip Shot

The first golf magazine, "Golf: A Weekly Record of 'Ye Royal and Ancient' Game", appeared in Great Britain in 1890.

QUIZ ANSWER: The Western Open, first contested in 1899

MAY 20th

TODAY'S THOUGHT: "I once played with Henry Ford II and told him you can buy a country, but you can't buy a golf swing. It's not on the shelf." —*Gene Sarazen*

HISTORY: On this date in 1962 Patty Berg won the 57th title of her career, finishing four-under-par at the Muskogee Civitan Open.

QUIZ: By what nickname did golfing legend Bobby Jones call his putter?

Chip Shot

Patty Berg's hole-in-one in the 1959 U.S. Women's Open made her the first woman to record an ace in USGA competition.

QUIZ ANSWER: Calamity Jane

MAY 21st

TODAY'S THOUGHT: "I wouldn't hurt a chicken crossing the road, but if I got a man in trouble on the golf course I'd kick the hell out of him. I don't care if he's my best friend." —*Sam Snead*

HISTORY: On this date in 1961 the Sam Snead Golf Festival tournament in White Sulphur Springs, WV was won by...Sam Snead.

QUIZ: 1966 was the first year the British Open was played over four days. What American came home with the title?

Chip Shot
In 1958 Snead won $14,000 in PGA purses. In 1959 his take from the TV show, "All-Star Golf", was $29,500.

QUIZ ANSWER: Jack Nicklaus

MAY 22nd

TODAY'S THOUGHT: "On tour, you've got to realize that if you take an eight on a hole, ninety percent of the other pros don't care and the other ten percent wish it had been a nine." —*Mason Rudolph*

HISTORY: On this date in 1994 Tom Lehman shot his fourth straight round of 67 in an easy five-stroke win at The Memorial. It was Lehman's first Tour win.

QUIZ: What tournament was Chip Beck playing in when he shot his record-tying round of 59?

Chip Shot
It's not that I cheat at golf. I play for my health, and a low score makes me feel better.

QUIZ ANSWER: The 1991 Las Vegas International

MAY 23rd

TODAY'S THOUGHT: "You can shoot lions in the dark and yet you can quiver like a leaf and fall flat over a two-foot putt." — *Johnny Farrell*

HISTORY: On this date in 1993 Bob Charles became the first golfer to earn $4 million on the Senior PGA Tour, winning the Bell Atlantic Classic.

QUIZ: Who won the Vardon Trophy for best scoring average in 1977, '78 and '79?

Chip Shot

Twice as many people visit Florida for a golf vacation as any other two states combined.

QUIZ ANSWER: Tom Watson

MAY 24th

TODAY'S THOUGHT: "A secret disbelief in the enemy's play is very useful for match play."—*Sir Walter Simpson*

HISTORY: On this date in 1987 Jane Geddes won the LPGA Championship and $52,500. Five years later, Pat Bradley earned $200,000...on one hole! Bradley sank a birdie putt in a skins game to win her paycheck.

QUIZ: Who is the oldest winner of the British Open?

Chip Shot

Gary Player remains the last golfer to win three tournaments in a row. But those three wins in 1978 were his last on the PGA Tour.

QUIZ ANSWER: Old Tom Morris, 46 years old in 1867

MAY 25th

TODAY'S THOUGHT: "Ben Hogan would rather have a coral snake rolling in his shirt than hit a hook."
—*Claude Harmon*

HISTORY: On this date in 1948 Ben Hogan defeated Mike Turnesa in match play to win the PGA Championship.

QUIZ: True or false? PGA Tour player Scott Verplank once won the NCAA championship as a member of the Oklahoma State golf team.

Chip Shot

At the 1964 PGA Championship, Arnold Palmer became the first golfer to shoot four sub-70 rounds in a major. But he still finished second.

QUIZ ANSWER: True. Verplank won it in 1986.

MAY 26th

TODAY'S THOUGHT: "We know a lot about the swing, one college golf coach said to me, but not much about how to help golfers learn it."
—*W. Timothy Gallwey, writer*

HISTORY: On this date in 1991 Betsy King scored six birdies and no bogeys in the final round to win the LPGA Corning Classic by six shots.

QUIZ: What Japanese golfer was named LPGA Player of the Year in 1987?

Chip Shot

"Champagne" Tony Lema got his nickname when he promised the press champagne instead of beer if he won the 1962 Orange County Open.

QUIZ ANSWER: Ayako Okamoto

MAY 27th

TODAY'S THOUGHT: "Forget your opponents; always play against par." —*Sam Snead*

HISTORY: On this date in 1912 "Slammin'" Sammy Snead was born. Snead recorded 81 victories on the PGA Tour, including seven majors.

QUIZ: Roberto DeVicenzo, who signed an incorrect scorecard to lose the 1968 Masters, did win one major. Which one?

Chip Shot

At the 1939 U.S. Open, Snead needed a par-five on the last hole to win by one stroke. He thought he needed a birdie, however, and hit into the rough and two bunkers before three putting for an eight. He lost by two strokes.

QUIZ ANSWER: DeVicenzo won the 1967 British Open.

MAY 28th

TODAY'S THOUGHT: "The Masters is Scarborough Fair, the gathering of eagles. Everyone wants to make the trip to Mecca." —*Bobby Jones*

HISTORY: On this date in 1991 the often-controversial Horn Hardin resigned as chairman of the Augusta National Golf Club.

QUIZ: The first Curtis Cup was held in 1932. But it wasn't until years later that the American women amateurs lost a match on their home ground. What year did they suffer their first loss?

Chip Shot

Jack Nicklaus is the only six-time winner of The Masters. He's also the only golfer to win the tournament five times.

QUIZ ANSWER: In 1986 the U.S. lost to Britain.

MAY 29th

TODAY'S THOUGHT: "I would rather play Hamlet with no rehearsal than play golf on television."
—*Jack Lemmon*

HISTORY: On this date in 1977 Sue Press made the history books when she became the first woman to hit consecutive holes-in-one. Press aced the 13th and 14th holes at the Chatswood Golf Club in Sydney, Australia.

QUIZ: Excluding Antarctica, which continent has the fewest golfers and golf courses?

Chip Shot
Golf is played in the United States at least once a year by over 20 million people on more than 12,400 courses.

QUIZ ANSWER: South America

MAY 30th

TODAY'S THOUGHT: "From being a kid it has been my dream to leave a legacy. I want people to say 'Did you see Nick Faldo play?'" —*Nick Faldo*

HISTORY: On this date in 1937 Denny Shute won his second straight PGA Championship when he defeated Harold McSpaden in the final round.

QUIZ: She lost the U.S. Women's Open in 1957 because she turned in an incorrect scorecard and was disqualified. Who was she?

Chip Shot
Club pro Craig Thomas' joy at qualifying for the 1993 Buick Open turned to embarrassment when he fired a whopping 92 in the first round.

QUIZ ANSWER: Jacqueline Pung

MAY 31st

 TODAY'S THOUGHT: "Here we are, making thousands of dollars a year, and we're trying to change our swings." —*Johnny Miller*

HISTORY: On this date in 1942 Sam Snead won the first major title of his career, topping Jim Turnesa in the PGA Championship.

QUIZ: You're my caddie as we head into the back nine of The Masters. I ask you to give me my baffy. What club will you hand me?

Chip Shot

The winner of the AT&T Pebble Beach National Pro-Am is awarded a 58-piece suite of crystal made by Waterford as well as a replica of the tournament trophy.

QUIZ ANSWER: The 5-wood

JUNE 1st

TODAY'S THOUGHT: "Golf combines two favorite American pastimes: taking long walks and hitting things with a stick." —*P.J. O'Rourke, writer*

HISTORY: On this date in 1986 Pat Bradley became the first golfer to win all four LPGA majors in her career. Bradley ran away from the field for an 11-stroke victory in the LPGA Championship.

QUIZ: Who were the first two golfers elected to the Woman's Hall of Fame?

Chip Shot

In 1990 Rob MacGregor bounced a golf ball on the face of his sand wedge a record-setting 3,699 times. The old record was held by Mark Mooney, who did it 1,764 times.

QUIZ ANSWER: Patty Berg and Babe Zaharias

JUNE 2nd

TODAY'S THOUGHT: "All the golf swing is, is two turns and a swish." —*Mary Bryan*

HISTORY: On this date in 1985 Nancy Lopez won her second LPGA Championship, this time by eight strokes. Lopez never missed a fairway on her way to an 8-stroke win.

QUIZ: Who is the only African-American golfer to have won the Vardon Trophy for scoring average?

Chip Shot

In a full drive by an average adult male golfer, the clubhead swings through the ball at about 100 mph. In contrast, PGA Tour players range from about 115 to 135 mph.

QUIZ ANSWER: Calvin Peete, who won the trophy in 1984

JUNE 3rd

 TODAY'S THOUGHT: "If you work very hard, they call you lucky. When they call you lucky, you know you're good." —*Chi Chi Rodriguez*

HISTORY: On this date in 1984 Patty Sheehan successfully defended her LPGA Championship. Sheehan tamed the Jack Nicklaus Golf Club course to finish 15-under-par and ten strokes ahead of runners-up Beth Daniel and Pat Bradley.

QUIZ: What golfer won four consecutive PGA Championships?

Chip Shot
Arnold Palmer's first PGA Tour check came at the 1955 Indiana Open. It was a modest $142.

QUIZ ANSWER: Walter Hagen, 1924-27

JUNE 4th

 TODAY'S THOUGHT: "I've seen better swings in a condemned playground." —*Arnold Palmer, to Bob Hope*

HISTORY: On this date in 1927 the United States and Great Britain faced off in the first Ryder Cup competition. The U.S. won, 9-1/2 to 2-1/2.

QUIZ: What Senior PGA Tour player scored eight straight birdies in the 1987 Silver Pages Classic?

Chip Shot
A pair of brass clubheads recovered in the 1970's from a Dutch ship that had sunk in 1653 were sold at auction in 1989. The price? $14,000 each.

QUIZ ANSWER: Chi Chi Rodriguez

JUNE 5th

TODAY'S THOUGHT: "My worst day on the golf course still beats my best day in the office."
—*John Hallisey, writer*

HISTORY: On this date in 1925 Scottish pro Willie Macfarlane upset amateur Bobby Jones by one stroke to win the U.S. Open.

QUIZ: Cary Middlecoff and Lloyd Mangrum endured the longest sudden-death playoff in history in the 1949 Motor City Open. Who won?

Chip Shot
Willie Macfarlane was the first U.S. Open champion to win wearing eyeglasses.

QUIZ ANSWER: Both were declared co-winners when darkness halted play after 11 holes.

JUNE 6th

TODAY'S THOUGHT: "Good night, this game teaches you a lot about yourself. You can tell by the way a guy walks how he's doing." —*Ben Crenshaw*

HISTORY: On this date in 1992 Arizona State left-hander Phil Mickelson won his third NCAA golf title. Mickelson joined Ben Crenshaw as the only two golfers to win three national titles.

QUIZ: What golfer holds the record for the most consecutive years on the top ten money-winning list?

Chip Shot
The trophy of the BellSouth Classic is a bronze replica of the Vardon grip. The model for the cast was Bobby Jones.

QUIZ ANSWER: Jack Nicklaus, 17 times, from 1962 to 1978

JUNE 7th

TODAY'S THOUGHT: "Good golfing temperament falls between taking it with a grin or shrug and throwing a fit." —*Sam Snead*

HISTORY: On this date in 1952 the Britain-Ireland team won the Curtis Cup from the United States. The victory was the team's first.

QUIZ: Legal or illegal? My ball accidentally hits my golf cart.

Chip Shot

On a hot summer day at the 1986 Anheuser Busch Golf Classic, Bill Kratzert had to withdraw from the event because he ran out of balls. His caddie, trying to lighten the golf bag, didn't bring enough extra balls!

QUIZ ANSWER: Illegal. It's a two-stroke penalty.

JUNE 8th

TODAY'S THOUGHT: "The wit of man has never invented a pastime equal to golf for its healthful recreation, its pleasurable excitement and its never-ending source of amusement."
—*A.J. Balfour, British prime minister*

HISTORY: On this date in 1980 Sally Little won her first career major, taking the LPGA Championship.

QUIZ: What Senior PGA Tour player holds the record for most consecutive years winning at least one tournament?

Chip Shot

Mary Queen of Scots was publicly criticized in 1567 for playing golf so soon after her husband was murdered.

QUIZ ANSWER: Miller Barber, from 1981-1989

JUNE 9th

TODAY'S THOUGHT: "Golf fans have a remarkable sixth sense that tells them what is happening elsewhere on the course, often a mile away. Some sort of telepathic wizardry takes place." —*Dan Hruby, writer*

HISTORY: On this date in 1991 Billy Andrade followed his career-first win at the Kemper Open with a two-stroke victory in the Buick Classic.

QUIZ: What school has won the most NCAA Team Golf Championships?

Chip Shot

An Australian tournament sponsor, a funeral director, once offered a prepaid funeral to anyone scoring an ace on a designated hole. Talk about a buried lie!

QUIZ ANSWER: Yale has won it 21 times.

JUNE 10th

TODAY'S THOUGHT: "Golf is so popular simply because it is the best game in the world at which to be bad." —*A.A. Milne, writer*

HISTORY: On this date in 1977 Al Geiberger holed an eight-foot putt on the final hole of the second round of the Memphis Classic to become the first golfer to shoot a round of 59. Geiberger went on to win the tournament.

QUIZ: How is golfer J.C. Snead related to the great Sam Snead?

Chip Shot

The only videotape of Geiberger's round was destroyed in a fire at the TV station that had the filmed record.

QUIZ ANSWER: J.C. is Sam's nephew.

JUNE 11th

TODAY'S THOUGHT: "I never wanted to be a millionaire. I just wanted to live like one."
—*Walter Hagen*

HISTORY: On this date in 1919 the first postwar U.S. Open was won by Walter Hagen in a playoff with Mike Brady. The Open had not been held in 1917 and '18.

QUIZ: I won the 1973 U.S. Open, the 1976 British Open and was PGA Player of the Year in 1974. Who am I?

Chip Shot

The night before the playoff, Hagen went to the theater and, later, socialized with the star of the show, Al Jolson. Hagen faced Brady with less than three hours of sleep.

QUIZ ANSWER: Johnny Miller

JUNE 12th

TODAY'S THOUGHT: "The Open is simply the Kentucky Derby, the Indy 500 and the Rose Bowl of its sport." —*Dan Jenkins, writer*

HISTORY: On this date in 1939 Byron Nelson won the only U.S. Open title of his career. The 26-year old Nelson beat Craig Wood in a playoff.

QUIZ: Who holds the PGA record for career holes-in-one?

Chip Shot

In 1946 Nelson was in the hunt for his second U.S. Open title when his caddy lost his balance and kicked Nelson's ball. That cost Nelson a penalty stroke which came back to haunt him. He eventually lost the title in a three-way playoff.

QUIZ ANSWER: Art Wall, Jr., with 37 career aces

JUNE 13th

TODAY'S THOUGHT: "The U.S. Open eliminates a lot of players. Some players just weren't made to win the U.S. Open. Quite often, a lot of them know it."
—*Jack Nicklaus*

HISTORY: On this date in 1953 Ben Hogan won his record-tying fourth U.S. Open.

QUIZ: Ben Hogan, Bobby Jones and Willie Anderson won four U.S. Opens. A fourth golfer has also done it. Who is he?

Chip Shot
'53 was a good year for Hogan. He also won The Masters and the British Open.

QUIZ ANSWER: Jack Nicklaus, who won the tournament in 1962, '67, '72 and '80

JUNE 14th

TODAY'S THOUGHT: "But when he saw a chance at the bacon hanging over the last green, he could put as much fire and fury into a finishing round of golf as Jack Dempsey could into a fight."
—*Bobby Jones, on Gene Sarazen*

HISTORY: On this date in 1922 Gene Sarazen won the PGA Championship, the first of two straight titles.

QUIZ: This golfer won nine tournaments in his rookie year, but is best remembered as the winner of the first Masters. Who is he?

Chip Shot
The National Association of Left-Handed Golfers has over 1,250 members. It's headquartered in Houston, Texas.

QUIZ ANSWER: Horton Smith

JUNE 15th

TODAY'S THOUGHT: "Trying to catch Jack Nicklaus from eight shots back is like trying to climb Mt. Everest in street shoes." —*Tom Kite*

HISTORY: On this date in 1980 Jack Nicklaus won his fourth U.S. Open championship. His total of 272 broke his own record by three strokes. An opening round 63 tied the mark set by Johnny Miller.

QUIZ: Sam Trahan, Mike McGee, Kenny Knox and Andy North share the record of 18 for the fewest in a round. Fewest what?

Chip Shot
The sixth green at the Riviera CC in Los Angeles was designed with a bunker in the middle of it.

QUIZ ANSWER: Putts

JUNE 16th

TODAY'S THOUGHT: "You must expect anything in golf. A stranger comes through, he's keen for a game, he seems affable enough, and on the eighth fairway he turns out to be an idiot." —*Alistair Cooke, writer*

HISTORY: On this date in 1968 Lee Trevino topped defending champ Jack Nicklaus by four strokes to win his first U.S. Open.

QUIZ: Name the only major championship Byron Nelson didn't win.

Chip Shot
In that Open, Trevino shot rounds of 69, 68, 69 and 69 to become the first in Open history to play four sub-70 rounds.

QUIZ ANSWER: Nelson never won the British Open.

JUNE 17th

TODAY'S THOUGHT: "Nobody wins the Open. It wins you." —*Dr. Cary Middlecoff, on the U.S. Open*

HISTORY: On this date in 1973 Johnny Miller shot a final round 63 at the Oakmont CC to come from six strokes back to win the U.S. Open. Twenty-one years later to the day, at the same course, Arnold Palmer announced his retirement, saying he'd still play in an occasional tournament.

QUIZ: Why do we call Cary Middlecoff "Doctor"?

Chip Shot

Palmer was introduced to championship golf at Oakmont in 1942 at the age of 12.

QUIZ ANSWER: Before turning pro Middlecoff was a dentist.

JUNE 18th

TODAY'S THOUGHT: "If you can't outplay them, outwork them." —*Ben Hogan*

HISTORY: On this date in 1960 Arnie's Army got bigger as Arnold Palmer came from seven strokes back to win his first U.S. Open.

QUIZ: This woman was the leading money winner on the LPGA Tour a record eight times. Do you know who she is?

Chip Shot

Nicklaus' playing partner for that final round was 47-year old Ben Hogan. Hogan finished two strokes behind Nicklaus.

QUIZ ANSWER: Kathy Whitworth, who earned $1,719,804 in her career

JUNE 19th

TODAY'S THOUGHT: "The Lord answers my prayers everywhere except on the golf course."
—Reverend Billy Graham

HISTORY: On this date in 1954 nearly 40,000 people were on hand at Baltusrol to watch Ed Furgol win the U.S. Open.

QUIZ: Only one golfer has been able to win two straight U.S. Opens at Baltusrol GC. Who is he?

Chip Shot

Besides being the first tournament to rope off the fairways, the '54 championship was the first to be televised nationally.

QUIZ ANSWER: Jack Nicklaus, who won the championship at Baltusrol in 1967 and again in 1980

JUNE 20th

TODAY'S THOUGHT: "Golf is a game of expletives not deleted." *—Irving A. Gladstone, writer*

HISTORY: On this date in 1964 Ken Venturi overcame 100 degree temperatures to win his first major at the U.S. Open. Thirty years later to the day, Ernie Els won the Open for his first victory in a major championship.

QUIZ: Name the state where Shinnecock Hills GC is located.

Chip Shot

Venturi's heat prostration prompted the USGA to change the format of the tournament to one round per day the following year.

QUIZ ANSWER: New York — More precisely, Southampton, NY

JUNE 21st

TODAY'S THOUGHT: "I've been out here fourteen years and I've never played in a U.S. Open. Jack Nicklaus points his year toward the major championships. I point away from them." —*Gary McCord*

HISTORY: On this date in 1981 David Graham became the first Australian to win the U.S. Open.

QUIZ: True or false? Senior PGA Tour golfer Jay Sigel never played on the regular Tour, but did win two U.S. Amateur titles.

Chip Shot
Woodrow Wilson was on the golf course in 1915 when he was informed of the sinking of the "Lusitania".

QUIZ ANSWER: True. He was top amateur in 1982 and '83.

JUNE 22nd

TODAY'S THOUGHT: "I called my neighbor, who is an avid golfer in the sense that if he had to choose between playing golf and achieving world peace, he'd want to know how many holes." —*Dave Barry, writer*

HISTORY: On this date in 1958 Patty Berg was the winner, once again, at the Western Open. It marked the seventh time that Berg won this major.

QUIZ: Patty Berg was one of four founders of the LPGA in 1950. Can you name the other three?

Chip Shot
Real golfers don't cry when they line up their fourth putt.

QUIZ ANSWER: Betty Jameson, Louise Suggs and Babe Zaharias

JUNE 23rd

TODAY'S THOUGHT: "I'm not like these young stars. I just throw some junk in the air and hope it stays out of the rough and eventually gets to the green."
—*Julius Boros*

HISTORY: On this date in 1963 Arnold Palmer lost a playoff at the U.S. Open for the second straight year. Julius Boros beat Palmer and Jacky Cupit.

QUIZ: Who was the first golfer to successfully defend her title at the U.S. Women's Open?

Chip Shot

To mark the 50th anniversary of Francis Ouimet's victory, the Open returned to the Brookline CC in Massachusetts.

QUIZ ANSWER: Mickey Wright, who won in 1958 and '59

JUNE 24th

TODAY'S THOUGHT: "These younger players all think they're so much better. Good grief. Maybe they are."
—*Shelley Hamlin*

HISTORY: On this date in 1968 Sandra Post became the first rookie to win the LPGA Championship.

QUIZ: Can you name the famous four courses that are clustered on the Monterey (CA) peninsula?

Chip Shot

The original plans for Augusta National included a par-three 19th hole, where the loser of a match could try to recoup his losses in a double-or-nothing bet. It was never built.

QUIZ ANSWER: Cypress Point, Pebble Beach, Monterey Peninsula and Spyglass Hill

JUNE 25th

TODAY'S THOUGHT: "This putting is wicked. It is sinful." —*James Braid, five-time British Open winner*

HISTORY: On this date in 1921 Jock Hutchinson became the first American to win the British Open. Hutchinson, who was St. Andrews born and bred, had moved to Chicago twenty years earlier.

QUIZ: Can you name the two golf courses where the most British Opens have been held?

Chip Shot

Bobby Jones made his first appearance at the Open that year, but played so poorly that he quit in the third round.

QUIZ ANSWER: St. Andrews and the Prestwick Golf Course

JUNE 26th

TODAY'S THOUGHT: "Eighteen holes of match play will teach you more about your foe than 19 years of dealing with him across a desk."
—*Grantland Rice, writer*

HISTORY: On this date in 1914 Babe Didrikson was born. The Texas native went on to win ten major golf championships.

QUIZ: Besides Jack Nicklaus, what golfer won two Masters in the '70's?

Chip Shot

Didrikson was a versatile athlete. In addition to golf she excelled in track and field, winning gold medals in the 800-meter hurdles and the javelin throw in the 1932 Olympics.

QUIZ ANSWER: Gary Player won it in 1974 and '78.

JUNE 27th

TODAY'S THOUGHT: "Hold up a one-iron and walk. Even God can't hit a one-iron."
—*Lee Trevino, on how to deal with lightning*

HISTORY: On this date in 1975 Lee Trevino, Jerry Heard and Bobby Nichols were struck by lightning in the second round of the Western Open. Only Heard was able to return to play, finishing fourth in the tournament.

QUIZ: What does the phrase "through the green" mean?

Chip Shot
A golfer blames fate for his bogies, but when he makes a birdie, he's personally responsible.

QUIZ ANSWER: It means the entire golf course except the teeing ground, the putting green and all hazards.

JUNE 28th

TODAY'S THOUGHT: "If you're stupid enough to whiff, you should be smart enough to forget it."
—*Arnold Palmer*

HISTORY: On this date in 1992 Gibby Gilbert won a golf tournament for the first time since 1977. Gilbert went wire-to-wire to take the Southwestern Bell Classic on the Senior PGA Tour.

QUIZ: This golfer won the U.S. Amateur in 1974 and, two years later, was the U.S. Open champion. Name him.

Chip Shot
Players at the Kampala Golf Club in Uganda are cautioned to avoid the water hazards because of crocodiles.

QUIZ ANSWER: Jerry Pate

JUNE 29th

TODAY'S THOUGHT: "You win because you are the last one to fall on your face." —*Val Skinner*

HISTORY: On this date in 1957 Jacqueline Pung's worst nightmare came true. Pung was low scorer at the U.S. Women's Open, but signed an incorrect scorecard. Betsy Rawls was declared the winner.

QUIZ: How frequently are the Ryder Cup matches held?

Chip Shot

Spectators, feeling sorry for Pung, passed the hat and collected $3,000 for her, $1,200 more than the first prize.

QUIZ ANSWER: Ryder Cup matches are held every other year on a home-and-home basis.

JUNE 30th

TODAY'S THOUGHT: "There's something haunting about getting up at dawn and walking a golf course, checking pin placements. It's easy to lose track of reality." —*Ernest "Creamy" Carolan, caddie*

HISTORY: On this date in 1991 Meg Mallon dropped in a ten-foot birdie putt on the final hole of the LPGA Championship to win her first major title.

QUIZ: The lowest scoring average for a season by an LPGA player is 70.73 strokes. Who did it?

Chip Shot

Real golfers have two handicaps: one for braggin' and one for bettin'.

QUIZ ANSWER: Nancy Lopez, in 1985

JULY 1st

TODAY'S THOUGHT: "Anyone who criticizes a golf course is like a person invited to a house for dinner who, on leaving, tells the host that the food was lousy."
—*Gary Player*

HISTORY: On this date in 1961 Mickey Wright won her third U.S. Women's Open title in four years, beating defending champ Betsy Rawls by six strokes.

QUIZ: Which of the major championships on the PGA Tour is held at the same golf course every year?

Chip Shot
The 107 yard, par-3 seventh hole at Pebble Beach GL is the shortest hole on the PGA Tour.

QUIZ ANSWER: The Masters, at Augusta National Golf Club

JULY 2nd

TODAY'S THOUGHT: "Every day I try to tell myself this is going to be fun today. I try to put myself in a great frame of mind before I go out — then I screw it up with the first shot." —*Johnny Miller*

HISTORY: On this date in 1967 Catherine Lacoste of France became the first and only amateur to take the U.S. Women's Open.

QUIZ: True or false? PGA Tour players Scott Simpson and Craig Stadler both attended the University of Southern California.

Chip Shot
The Chicago Golf Course in Wheaton, Illinois was the first 18-hole golf course. It was built in 1894.

QUIZ ANSWER: True

JULY 3rd

TODAY'S THOUGHT: "When I make a bad shot, your job is to take the blame."
—*Seve Ballesteros, to his caddies*

HISTORY: On this date in 1951 Sam Snead won the third PGA Championship of his career, beating Walter Burkemo, 7 & 6.

QUIZ: Four players have shot a round of 63 in the PGA Championship. How many can you name?

Chip Shot
The average PGA Tour caddie is paid $300-$400 a week plus 6 percent of his player's winnings.

QUIZ ANSWER: Bruce Crampton, 1975; Raymond Floyd, 1982; Gary Player, 1984; and Vijay Singh, 1993

JULY 4th

TODAY'S THOUGHT: "Golf is twenty percent mechanics and technique. The other eighty percent is philosophy, humor, tragedy, romance, melodrama, companionship, camaraderie, cussedness and conversation." —*Grantland Rice*

HISTORY: On this date in 1965 Carol Mann picked up the only major title of her career, shooting four-under-par to win the U.S. Women's Open.

QUIZ: Two golfers have won the Vare Trophy for low scoring average on the LPGA Tour five times. Who are they?

Chip Shot
Golf is a game which separates the men from the poise.

QUIZ ANSWER: Mickey Wright and JoAnne Carner

JULY 5th

TODAY'S THOUGHT: "The worst club in my bag is my brain." —*Chris Perry*

HISTORY: On this date in 1970 Donna Caponi became only the second golfer to defend her title in the U.S. Women's Open.

QUIZ: True or false? Byron Nelson won the 1943 U.S. Open.

Chip Shot

Hollywood stars presented the golfers to the gallery when Los Angeles hosted the PGA Championship in 1929. Actress Fay Wray introduced Walter Hagen as "the Opium Champion of Great Britain".

QUIZ ANSWER: False. The 1943 Open was never held.

JULY 6th

TODAY'S THOUGHT: "In other games you get another chance. In baseball you get three cracks at it; in tennis you lose only one point. But in golf the loss of one shot has been responsible for the loss of heart."
—*Tommy Armour*

HISTORY: On this date in 1959 two Hall of Famers battled to the end at the LPGA Championship. Betsy Rawls won her first title beating Patty Berg.

QUIZ: Legal or illegal? I swing at a ball and top it. When it's in the air my club strikes it a second time.

Chip Shot

Real golfers never question their client's score.

QUIZ ANSWER: Illegal, with a one-stroke penalty

JULY 7th

TODAY'S THOUGHT: "The person I fear in the last two rounds is myself." —*Tom Watson*

HISTORY: On this date in 1994 PGA Tour veteran Bob Lohr fired a 10-underpar 61 in the opening round of the Anheuser-Busch Golf Classic. The only scores better than the 61 were the 59's of Al Geiberger and Chip Beck and nine rounds of 60.

QUIZ: Name the golf club that hosted the first U.S. Open in 1895.

Chip Shot

In 1973 Arthur Thompson shot a round of 103 at the Uplands Golf Course in British Columbia. Not bad for a man who was 103 years old.

QUIZ ANSWER: The Newport (RI) Golf Club

JULY 8th

TODAY'S THOUGHT: "There are no points for style when it comes to putting. It's getting the ball to drop that counts." —*Brian Swarbrick, writer*

HISTORY: On this date in 1976 Fuzzy Zoeller was red-hot as he fired off eight consecutive birdies in the first round of the Quad Cities Open.

QUIZ: In what decade did the Walker Cup matches begin?

Chip Shot

Only one golfer has shot two holes-in-one in British Open competition. Charles Ward aced the eighth at St. Andrews in 1946 and, two years later, the 13th at Muirfield.

QUIZ ANSWER: The 1920's — The first match was in 1922.

JULY 9th

TODAY'S THOUGHT: "I enjoyed playing in the last group behind Jack Nicklaus. Only trouble was the tournament director kept taking the pins off the greens once Nicklaus played through." —*Lou Graham*

HISTORY: On this date in 1966 Jack Nicklaus conquered Muirfield to win his first British Open. With the win Nicklaus joined Gene Sarazen, Ben Hogan and Gary Player, the only men to win all four majors.

QUIZ: Who has won more British Open titles, Jack Nicklaus or Gary Player?

Chip Shot
Nicklaus was a member of the 1959 Walker Cup team when he made his only previous visit to Muirfield.

QUIZ ANSWER: Both have won three championships.

JULY 10th

TODAY'S THOUGHT: "You can talk to a fade, but a hook won't listen." —*Lee Trevino*

HISTORY: On this date in 1971 Lee Trevino won his first British Open championship.

QUIZ: I am the only U.S. Junior Amateur champion to go on and win the U.S. Open. These days, the bulk of my work is done behind a microphone instead of behind a putter. Who am I?

Chip Shot
American J.J. McDermott wanted to play in the 1914 British Open, but when he arrived in England, he discovered that he was a week late for qualifying.

QUIZ ANSWER: Johnny Miller

JULY 11th

TODAY'S THOUGHT: "You may cry in victory, but don't ever cry in defeat again."
—*Mrs. Venturi, Ken's mom*

HISTORY: On this date in 1993 Tom Weiskopf was back in Jack Nicklaus' shadow. Weiskopf, a two-time runner-up to Nicklaus in The Masters, was one stroke behind him in the U.S. Senior Open.

QUIZ: Who was the first LPGA golfer to earn over $100,000 in a season?

Chip Shot
Craig Wood won the 1941 U.S. Open, but was unable to defend his title for five years. After America entered WWII, the USGA canceled all championships for the duration.

QUIZ ANSWER: Judy Rankin, with $150,734 in 1976

JULY 12th

TODAY'S THOUGHT: "Don't make it happen, let it happen." —*Bob Rotella, sports psychologist*

HISTORY: On this date in 1930 Bobby Jones became the first golfer to break par in the U.S. Open and, as a result, won his fourth Open title.

QUIZ: What is Paul Runyan's claim to fame, other than winning the PGA Championship two times?

Chip Shot
Jones was feeling the pressure of the Grand Slam. During that Open, Jones lost 14 pounds.

QUIZ ANSWER: Runyan was the PGA Tour's first official leading money-winner. He took in $6,767 in 1934.

JULY 13th

TODAY'S THOUGHT: "After taking the stance, it is too late to worry. The only thing to do then is to hit the ball." —*Bobby Jones*

HISTORY: On this date in 1980 Amy Alcott fought off 100-degree temperatures in Nashville to win the U.S. Women's Open.

QUIZ: True or false? Byron Nelson won the first Byron Nelson Golf Classic.

Chip Shot

The only time a son succeeded a father as champion of a major was when Old Tom Morris won the 1867 British Open and Young Tom Morris won the title in 1868.

QUIZ ANSWER: False. The event previously was known as the Dallas Classic.

JULY 14th

TODAY'S THOUGHT: "I never had a good bounce. All I ever had were bad ones." —*Arnold Palmer*

HISTORY: On this date in 1991 two weeks after winning the LPGA Championship, Meg Mallon fired three birdies on the back nine on her way to winning the U.S. Women's Open.

QUIZ: You're my caddie as I play the back nine of the British Open. I ask for my "jigger". What club do you hand me?

Chip Shot

If your dream is to see The Masters in person, wake up. The waiting list for tickets was closed in 1978.

QUIZ ANSWER: The 4-iron

JULY 15th

TODAY'S THOUGHT: "Advice is seldom welcome. Those who need it the most always like it the least." —*The Earl of Chesterfield*

HISTORY: On this date in 1923 Bobby Jones finally put his name on the list of major tournament winners with a victory in the U.S. Open.

QUIZ: Was Nick Faldo the first golfer to use a female caddie while playing in The Masters?

Chip Shot
Jones was a grizzled veteran of major tournaments despite his young age. He had been trying for a major since age 14.

QUIZ ANSWER: No. George Archer's daughter caddied for him in the 1983 tournament.

JULY 16th

TODAY'S THOUGHT: "Golf is a nonviolent game played violently from within." —*Bob Toski*

HISTORY: On this date in 1993 Nick Faldo shattered the course record at Royal St. George's in the second round of the British Open. Faldo's 63 was three strokes better than anyone else could manage.

QUIZ: Of the four major championships, what is the only one Walter Hagen didn't win in his career?

Chip Shot
A golf cart is started and stopped an average of 150 times during a round of golf.

QUIZ ANSWER: Hagen never won The Masters.

JULY 17th

TODAY'S THOUGHT: "The terrible thing about a missed shot in golf is that the thing is done, irrevocably, irretrievably. Perhaps that is why golf is so great a game; it is so much like the game of life. We don't have the shots over in either."
—*O.B. Keeler, writer*

HISTORY: On this date in 1955 Beverly Hanson won the first LPGA Championship.

QUIZ: What is a stymie?

Chip Shot

My golf game has been so bad, I'm just gonna buy a bucket of balls and practice my drop.

QUIZ ANSWER: An intentional putt between an opponent's ball and the hole without marking the ball

JULY 18th

TODAY'S THOUGHT: "It's a silly game where nobody wins." —*Thomas Fuller, writer, on golf*

HISTORY: On this date in 1993 Greg Norman, playing the best golf of his life, captured his second British Open title. Norman's four-round score of 267 was the lowest score in the championship's 122 years.

QUIZ: Name the two golfers Fuzzy Zoeller beat in a playoff to win the 1979 Masters.

Chip Shot

Until Norman's victory, only one other winner had broken par in twelve Opens held at Royal St. George's.

QUIZ ANSWER: Ed Sneed and Tom Watson

JULY 19th

TODAY'S THOUGHT: "I thank the press from the heart of my, well, bottom."
—*Nick Faldo, after the 1992 British Open*

HISTORY: On this date in 1992 Nick Faldo squandered a four-stroke lead, but came back to win his third British Open.

QUIZ: What American won the British Open five times?

Chip Shot

The golf clubs of Presidents Warren Harding, William Howard Taft, Franklin D. Roosevelt and Woodrow Wilson are on display at the Burning Tree Club in Bethesda, MD.

QUIZ ANSWER: Tom Watson

JULY 20th

TODAY'S THOUGHT: "Golf is just the old-fashioned pool hall moved outdoors, but with no chairs around the walls." —*Will Rogers*

HISTORY: On this date in 1958 Dow Finsterwald won the first PGA Championship conducted as a stroke play, not match play, event.

QUIZ: Name the other golfer who, like Nicklaus, won the PGA Championship five times.

Chip Shot

Only one golfer has won the PGA Championship more than two times since it moved to stroke play. Jack Nicklaus has done it five times.

QUIZ ANSWER: Walter Hagen

JULY 21st

TODAY'S THOUGHT: "Golf's like life with the volume turned up." —*Mike Reid*

HISTORY: On this date in 1991 Ian Baker-Finch left nothing to chance in winning his first British Open. The Australian birdied five of the first seven holes.

QUIZ: In the 1983 British Open, this American missed a three-inch putt and eventually lost the championship by one stroke. Who was he?

Chip Shot

Richard Boxall was only three strokes behind the leaders when he stepped to the ninth tee in the third round. Boxall broke his leg while swinging and had to withdraw. His final tee shot, ironically, was right down the middle.

QUIZ ANSWER: Hale Irwin

JULY 22nd

TODAY'S THOUGHT: "I paid my dues. That's golfer-talk for hitting a million balls." —*Jim Thorpe*

HISTORY: On this date in 1984 Kathy Whitworth earned her 85th career win at the Rochester Open, passing Sam Snead as golf's winningest player.

QUIZ: This golfer won a Purple Heart in World War II, then came home and won the 1946 U.S. Open. Who was he?

Chip Shot

Between 1958 and 1978 Arnold Palmer, Jack Nicklaus and Gary Player won 38 percent of the 84 major championships played.

QUIZ ANSWER: Lloyd Mangrum

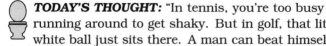

JULY 23rd

TODAY'S THOUGHT: "In tennis, you're too busy running around to get shaky. But in golf, that little white ball just sits there. A man can beat himself before he ever swings at it."
—*Ellsworth Vines, tennis champ turned golfer*

HISTORY: On this date in 1960 Betsy Rawls won her fourth U.S. Women's Open.

QUIZ: Name the last golfer to successfully defend her U.S. Women's Open title.

Chip Shot

JoAnn Washam is the only golfer to ace two holes in the same LPGA tournament. Washam did it in the second and final rounds of the 1979 Women's Kemper Open.

QUIZ ANSWER: Betsy King, who won in 1989 and '90

JULY 24th

TODAY'S THOUGHT: "I dropped off the tour and went home and started working with my Dad doing taxes. After two months of that, I decided golf looked pretty good." —*John Fought*

HISTORY: On this date in 1966 "Champagne" Tony Lema lost his life in a plane crash near Lansing, Michigan.

QUIZ: Since 1950 only one PGA golfer has been able to win more than ten tournaments in a year. Who was it?

Chip Shot

The plane in which the 1964 British Open winner was riding came down on the seventh green of a golf course.

QUIZ ANSWER: Sam Snead, who won 11 events in 1950

JULY 25th

TODAY'S THOUGHT: "My philosophy is: Never do anything stupid." —*Ben Crenshaw*

HISTORY: On this date in 1993 Lauri Merten ended a nine-year victory drought with a win in the U.S. Women's Open by one stroke.

QUIZ: This Hall of Fame golfer was named captain of the United States Ryder Cup 6 times, more than anyone else. Who is he?

Chip Shot

W.F. Davis of the Royal Montreal GC is acknowledged as North America's first greenkeeper. Hired as club pro in 1888, Davis was also expected to perform the duties of greenkeeper.

QUIZ ANSWER: Walter Hagen

JULY 26th

TODAY'S THOUGHT: "Golf is not a game you can rush. For every stroke you try to force out of her, she is going to extract two strokes in return." —*Dave Hill*

HISTORY: On this date in 1981 Pat Bradley added another major title to her resume with a win in the U.S. Women's Open.

QUIZ: Under USGA rules, how long can you look for a lost ball?

Chip Shot

Sam Snead didn't carry a putter in his bag until he went on the PGA Tour in 1937. His first set of clubs, purchased in the 1920's, cost him $9.50.

QUIZ ANSWER: 5 minutes

JULY 27th

TODAY'S THOUGHT: "If the following foursome is pressing you, wave them through and then speed up."
—*Deane Beman*

HISTORY: On this date in 1992 Patty Sheehan forced a playoff in the U.S. Women's Open by making two straight birdies on the final holes. Her third straight, on the first playoff hole, gave her the title over Julie Inkster.

QUIZ: What is a slice that starts left and then fades?

Chip Shot

Grantland Rice suggested that the first Masters, in 1934, be held in late March so baseball writers returning north from spring training could cover the tournament.

QUIZ ANSWER: A "banana ball"

JULY 28th

TODAY'S THOUGHT: "I try to have peace of mind. If you have that, you are a mental millionaire. It doesn't cost anything." —*Chi Chi Rodriguez*

HISTORY: On this date in 1987 the longest U.S. Women's Open came to an end with Laura Davies winning in a playoff. The event lasted six days because of the playoff and heavy thunderstorms.

QUIZ: What two Americans won back-to-back British Opens in the 1920's?

Chip Shot

After winning the 1949 LA Open, Lloyd Mangrum dropped his pants before the media to show why he won: lucky pajama bottoms, which he wore under his golf pants.

QUIZ ANSWER: Bobby Jones and Walter Hagen

JULY 29th

TODAY'S THOUGHT: "The average golfer doesn't play golf. He attacks it." —*Jackie Burke, Jr.*

HISTORY: On this date in 1991 Jack Nicklaus became the only man to win major USGA titles in five decades with a playoff victory over Chi Chi Rodriguez in the U.S. Senior Open.

QUIZ: This golfer posted the lowest score ever shot by an amateur at the U.S. Open when he shot a 282 in 1960. Do you know who it was?

Chip Shot

Nicklaus and Arnold Palmer are the only men to win the U.S. Amateur, the U.S. Open and the U.S. Senior Open.

QUIZ ANSWER: Jack Nicklaus

JULY 30th

TODAY'S THOUGHT: "There are two things in life which Ben Hogan especially dislikes. One is losing a golf match. The other is teaching golf."
—*Jimmy Demaret*

HISTORY: On this date in 1961 Jerry Barber survived a playoff with Don January to win the PGA Championship for the only major title of his career.

QUIZ: Name the trophy, donated by the son of a department store magnate, which is given to the winner of the PGA Championship.

Chip Shot

Barber, trailing by four strokes with three holes to play, birdied putts of 22, 44 and 58 feet.

QUIZ ANSWER: The Wanamaker Trophy

JULY 31st

TODAY'S THOUGHT: "Those who cannot drive suppose themselves to be good putters." —*Sir Walter Simpson*

HISTORY: On this date in 1983 Australian Jan Stephenson's victory in the U.S. Women's Open left her one short of a career grand slam. The Nabisco Dinah Shore is the only major to elude Stephenson.

QUIZ: Name the native country of 1963 British Open winner Bob Charles.

Chip Shot

After leading through 54 holes of the 1967 U.S. Open, amateur Marty Fleckman decided to turn pro. He won the Cajun Classic in his pro debut, but never won again.

QUIZ ANSWER: New Zealand

AUGUST 1st

TODAY'S THOUGHT: "I believe my future is ahead of me." —*Chip Beck, after his first PGA Tour win*

HISTORY: On this date in 1993 Nick Price won his fourth tournament of the year with a three-stroke victory in the Federal Express-St. Jude Classic.

QUIZ: I won the U.S. Open twice. Each time I won, a different brother of mine finished second. Who am I?

Chip Shot
At one point in 1991 and '92, Fred Couples won $2.5 million. As a result, his caddie, Joe LaCava, earned $200,000.

QUIZ ANSWER: Alex Smith, whose brother, Willie, was runner-up in 1906 while Macdonald Smith finished second in 1910

AUGUST 2nd

TODAY'S THOUGHT: "Golf is the hardest game in the world to play and the easiest to cheat at." —*Dave Hill*

HISTORY: On this date in 1959 Bob Rosburg overcame a six-stroke deficit by firing a final-round 66 to win the PGA Championship.

QUIZ: Name the only golfer to win consecutive British Open titles in the 1980's.

Chip Shot
Like the other majors, it's tough to repeat as champion of the PGA. Between 1950 and '70, no golfer won the event two years in a row.

QUIZ ANSWER: Tom Watson, in 1982 and 1983

AUGUST 3rd

TODAY'S THOUGHT: "The man who hates golfers is what they call me. They couldn't be more wrong. I design holes that are fun to play."
—Trent Jones, golf course designer

HISTORY: On this date in 1975 three players tied for second as Susie Berning won the Lady Keystone Classic.

QUIZ: The lowest score for 72 holes in an LPGA tournament is 268. Who is the golfer who set this record in 1985?

Chip Shot
Ray Ainsley shot a 19 on the 16th hole at Cherry Hills CC in the 1938 U.S. Open, a record that still stands.

QUIZ ANSWER: Nancy Lopez, at the Henredon Classic

AUGUST 4th

TODAY'S THOUGHT: "It's like eating. You don't think to feed yourself. All my concentration was on the scoring, not the swing, so I'll never know what caused it." *—Byron Nelson, on his winning streak*

HISTORY: On this date in 1945 Byron Nelson won the Canadian Open for his 11th straight tour victory, a record that still stands.

QUIZ: Two golfers were honored by "Sports Illustrated" with the magazine's Sportsman of the Year award in the 1970's. Can you name them?

Chip Shot
During a three year span, Nelson played in 75 tournaments, winning 35 of them.

QUIZ ANSWER: Lee Trevino and Jack Nicklaus

AUGUST 5th

TODAY'S THOUGHT: "Playing with your spouse on the golf course runs almost as great a marital risk as getting caught with someone else's anywhere else."
—*Peter Andrews, writer*

HISTORY: On this date in 1979 Nancy Lopez continued her domination of the LPGA, finishing 14-under-par to win the Colgate European Open.

QUIZ: In 1987 David Frost had the best scoring average on the PGA Tour, yet didn't win the Vardon Trophy. Why not?

Chip Shot
Laura Davies once won a long-driving competition by outhitting 40 men with a drive of 312 yards.

QUIZ ANSWER: Frost was not a member of the PGA.

AUGUST 6th

TODAY'S THOUGHT: "Patience. Patience and memory."
—*Art Wall, on what it takes to be a great golfer*

HISTORY: On this date in 1978 John Mahaffey put matters to rest when he dropped in a birdie putt on the second hole of sudden-death to win the PGA Championship. Mahaffey was tied with Tom Watson and Jerry Pate.

QUIZ: Who won the first PGA Championship in 1916?

Chip Shot
Byron Nelson chose the PGA Championship to make his final Tour appearance. Nelson played in the 1946 PGA.

QUIZ ANSWER: Jim Barnes

AUGUST 7th

TODAY'S THOUGHT: "It seems like everywhere we go this year, the galleries increase in size, and decrease in sanity." —*Pat Summerall, announcer*

HISTORY: On this date in 1983 second-year pro Hal Sutton held off Jack Nicklaus by one stroke to win the PGA Championship. Sutton finished the year as the tour's leading money-winner.

QUIZ: Legal or illegal? My ball is in the fairway and a loose twig is touching it. I pick up the twig and, in the process, my ball moves.

Chip Shot
When Julius Boros won the 1968 PGA Championship, he became the oldest man to take the event. Boros was 48.

QUIZ ANSWER: Illegal — a one-stroke penalty

AUGUST 8th

TODAY'S THOUGHT: "Golf is a fickle game and must be wooed to be won."
—*Willie Park, Jr., British Open champion*

HISTORY: On this date in 1982 Ray Floyd couldn't be stopped as he took home the PGA Championship. Floyd, who shot an opening round 63, led the event from start to finish.

QUIZ: True or false? Gary Player never won the PGA's Player of the Year award in his career.

Chip Shot
The largest collection of golf books in the world belongs to the USGA Museum and Library.

QUIZ ANSWER: True

AUGUST 9th

TODAY'S THOUGHT: "Golfers find it a very trying matter to turn at the waist, more particularly if they have a lot of waist to turn." *—Harry Vardon*

HISTORY: On this date in 1981 Larry Nelson's four-stroke lead held up for the final round as Nelson won his first major, the PGA Championship.

QUIZ: What golfer was the first to win a PGA Tour event with a yellow ball?

Chip Shot

Nelson's victory in the PGA earned him a berth on the Ryder Cup team, replacing the unfortunate Howard Twitty, who had already been measured for his Cup outfit.

QUIZ ANSWER: Wayne Levi won the 1982 Hawaiian Open.

AUGUST 10th

TODAY'S THOUGHT: "I've never played a perfect 18 holes. There's no such thing." *—Walter Hagen*

HISTORY: On this date in 1980 Jack Nicklaus joined Walter Hagen as the only five-time winners of the PGA Championship.

QUIZ: What is a "featherie"?

Chip Shot

One year the famous azaleas at Augusta National were blooming too early for the tournament. Workers packed ice around the plants to slow the process down.

QUIZ ANSWER: A golf ball used until about 1850, the featherie was a leather sack filled with wet goose feathers. When the feathers dried, they expanded and made the ball hard.

AUGUST 11th

TODAY'S THOUGHT: "Nothing goes down slower than a golf handicap." —*Bobby Nichols*

HISTORY: On this date in 1991 long-hitting and longshot rookie John Daly surprised everyone by winning the PGA Championship.

QUIZ: I won the U.S. Open in 1986. However, I competed in 22 Opens before finally winning. Who am I?

Chip Shot

Daly gained entry into the tournament when five players backed out, three alternates didn't make the trip and Nick Price withdrew when his wife was about to give birth.

QUIZ ANSWER: Raymond Floyd

AUGUST 12th

TODAY'S THOUGHT: "He has won more titles at more weights than Sugar Ray Leonard."
—*John Brodie, on the waistline of Billy Casper*

HISTORY: On this date in 1973 Jack Nicklaus' win in the PGA Championship gave him 14 major victories in his career, breaking the record held by Bobby Jones.

QUIZ: Orville Moody won only one major in his PGA career. Which one?

Chip Shot

When rain washed out the first two rounds of the 1983 Hong Kong Open, Greg Norman practiced by driving golf balls out the open window of his hotel room into the harbor.

QUIZ ANSWER: Moody won the 1969 U.S. Open.

AUGUST 13th

TODAY'S THOUGHT: "If I miss one day's practice I know it; if I miss two days the spectators know it; and if I miss three days the world knows it." —*Ben Hogan*

HISTORY: On this date in 1912 William Benjamin Hogan was born. Hogan, voted in 1973 as one of America's five greatest golfers, won nine majors in his career.

QUIZ: The first five British Opens played in England were played at two courses. Name them.

Chip Shot

When Hogan won the British Open at Carnoustie in 1953, the green fee was 49 cents.

QUIZ ANSWER: The Royal Liverpool GC and the Royal St. George's GC

AUGUST 14th

TODAY'S THOUGHT: "You've just one problem. You stand too close to the ball — after you've hit it."
—*Sam Snead, to a pupil*

HISTORY: On this date in 1977 the PGA Championship became the first major tournament to be decided in a sudden-death playoff. Lanny Wadkins beat Gene Littler on the third hole of the playoff.

QUIZ: Who was the first foreign-born player to win a million dollars in her career on the LPGA Tour?

Chip Shot

Bob Charles is known as the first left-hander to win a major tournament, the 1963 British Open.

QUIZ ANSWER: Australian Jan Stephenson

AUGUST 15th

TODAY'S THOUGHT: "You don't know what pressure is until you play for five bucks with only two in your pocket." —*Lee Trevino*

HISTORY: On this date in 1948 Babe Zaharias burst from the field to win the U.S. Women's Open by eight strokes.

QUIZ: I'm heading into Amen Corner at The Masters when I ask you, my caddie, to give me my trusty "spoon". What club do I want?

Chip Shot
After shooting a 77 in the first round of the 1974 U.S. Open, Homero Blancas was asked if he had had any uphill putts. Blancas replied, "Yeah, after each of my downhill putts."

QUIZ ANSWER: The 3-wood

AUGUST 16th

TODAY'S THOUGHT: "Real golfers go to work to relax." —*Anonymous*

HISTORY: On this date in 1992 Nick Price picked up the first major title of his career with a three-stroke victory in the PGA Championship, while Sherri Steinhauer captured the duMaurier Classic, the last major of the season on the LPGA Tour.

QUIZ: A number of players have won two majors in the same year. Name the two golfers who did it in the 1980's.

Chip Shot
Defending PGA Champ, John Daly, finished 20-over-par, 26 strokes behind Price.

QUIZ ANSWER: Jack Nicklaus and Tom Watson

AUGUST 17th

TODAY'S THOUGHT: "Great golf courses should have at least one silly hole." —*Frank Hannigan*

HISTORY: On this date in 1969 Raymond Floyd held off Gary Player by one stroke to win the PGA Championship, the first major win of his career.

QUIZ: This Swedish golfer's first victory on the LPGA Tour was at the 1988 U.S. Women's Open. That year she was named the Tour's Rookie of the Year. What's her name?

Chip Shot

For every doctor advising a patient to play golf, there's an instructor advising him to quit.

QUIZ ANSWER: Liselotte Neumann

AUGUST 18th

TODAY'S THOUGHT: "If there is any larceny in a man, golf will bring it out." —*Paul Gallico, writer*

HISTORY: On this date in 1957 Nick Faldo was born. Faldo, hooked on golf as a kid by television, gave TV viewers many memorable moments between 1987 and 1992 when he won three British Open titles and back-to-back Masters tournaments.

QUIZ: Name the golfer from Fiji who was named PGA Tour Rookie of the Year in 1993.

Chip Shot

Faldo won his two Masters in sudden-death playoffs.

QUIZ ANSWER: Vijay Singh

AUGUST 19th

TODAY'S THOUGHT: "I'd just as soon pull a rattlesnake out of my bag as a two-iron." —*Lee Trevino*

HISTORY: On this date in 1984 44-year old Lee Trevino won his first major in ten years, and sixth overall, taking the PGA Championship.

QUIZ: How many Vardon Trophies have Jack Nicklaus, Johnny Miller and Raymond Floyd won among them?

Chip Shot
King Hassan of Morocco had a nine-hole course built within the palace walls. Having trouble with the sand shot, the king ordered workers to fill in the 40 plus bunkers with sod.

QUIZ ANSWER: One — Raymond Floyd won it in 1983.

AUGUST 20th

TODAY'S THOUGHT: "I think most of the rules of golf stink. They were written by the guys who can't even break a hundred." —*Chi Chi Rodriguez*

HISTORY: On this date in 1944 a relative unknown from Indiana named Robert Hamilton upset Byron Nelson in the finals to win the PGA Championship.

QUIZ: Name the only two brothers who have each won more than $1.5 million in their careers on the PGA Tour.

Chip Shot
At that time, most of the top pros were fighting the war in Europe. Nelson was rejected by the Army because he was a hemophiliac.

QUIZ ANSWER: Bobby and Lanny Wadkins

AUGUST 21st

TODAY'S THOUGHT: "It has no rough, in the accepted sense of the term, and no semi-rough. Your ball is either on the fairway, in which case it sits invitingly on a flawless carpet of turf, or it is not."
—*Henry Longhurst, on Pine Valley*

HISTORY: On this date in 1971 16-year old Laura Baugh became the youngest golfer to win the U.S. Women's Amateur title when she beat Beth Barry.

QUIZ: Jack Nicklaus has won The Masters six times. Who's next on the list with four green jackets?

Chip Shot
Real golfers don't cry when they line up for their fourth putt.

QUIZ ANSWER: Arnold Palmer

AUGUST 22nd

TODAY'S THOUGHT: "When you start driving your ball down the middle, you meet a different class of people."
—*Phil Harris, comedian*

HISTORY: On this date in 1993 Phil Mickelson won his second tournament of the year with an easy victory in The International.

QUIZ: Who was the youngest winner of the British Open?

Chip Shot
The International uses a modified Stableford scoring system. Medal scores don't count. Instead, points are awarded for a player's performance on each hole.

QUIZ ANSWER: Young Tom Morris was 17 years old when he captured the Open in 1868.

AUGUST 23rd

TODAY'S THOUGHT: "Even the best swing doesn't work all the time. You have to be able to post a good number on those days when you can't even write your own damn name." —*Gardner Dickinson*

HISTORY: On this date in 1955 Hall of Famer Betty Jameson won the last LPGA title of her career, shooting 3-under-par to win the White Mountain Open.

QUIZ: What American city had the first muni, or municipal golf course?

Chip Shot

The BBC carried the British Open live for the first time in 1955, the year Peter Thomson won the second of five titles.

QUIZ ANSWER: New York City — Van Cortlandt GC was founded in the Bronx in 1895 and is still used.

AUGUST 24th

TODAY'S THOUGHT: "You show me a player who swings out of his shoes and I'll show you a player who isn't going to win enough to keep himself in a decent pair of shoes for very long." —*Sam Snead*

HISTORY: On this date in 1984 Pat Bradley set an LPGA record for nine holes, firing a 28 at the Columbia Savings Classic. Bradley finished the round at 65.

QUIZ: Who was the first foreign-born player to win The Masters?

Chip Shot

Bradley had the record all to herself for less than a week. Mary Beth Zimmerman shot a 28 at the Tour's next event, the Rail Charity Golf Classic.

QUIZ ANSWER: South African Gary Player, in 1961

AUGUST 25th

TODAY'S THOUGHT: "The only bruises in golf are to the spirit. The only bones that break are those in the skeleton of the personality." —*Thomas Boswell, writer*

HISTORY: On this date in 1991 Mitch Voges beat Manny Zerman in the title match of the U.S. Amateur Golf Championship.

QUIZ: What Senior PGA Tour golfer won back-to-back U.S. Amateur Golf Championships?

Chip Shot

After Ben Crenshaw sent his ball into a palm tree, his caddie climbed a ladder and shook the tree. Two dozen balls fell out, none of them belonging to Crenshaw.

QUIZ ANSWER: Jay Sigel, who won in 1982 and '83

AUGUST 26th

TODAY'S THOUGHT: "In Japan, player who scores hole-in-one while leading tournament always loses. It's proven jinx." —*Ayako Okamoto*

HISTORY: On this date in 1962 Mickey Wright won her third consecutive event, taking the Salt Lake City Open.

QUIZ: Who has won the U.S. Open in three different decades?

Chip Shot

Sam Snead was playing in a tournament on the day of the 1948 presidential election. As early returns started to come in, someone mentioned to Snead that Dewey was leading. "What'd he go out in?" Snead asked.

QUIZ ANSWER: Jack Nicklaus

AUGUST 27th

TODAY'S THOUGHT: "If you ever get a tee time in hell, there will be two certainties: l) You will be playing behind Bernhard Langer, and 2) The course will include Hazeltine's 16th." —*Rick Reilly, writer*

HISTORY: On this date in 1957 Bernhard Langer was born. Langer, known for his slow play, won the 1985 and 1993 Masters, but is remembered for the missed putt that gave the 1991 Ryder Cup to the U.S.

QUIZ: What's the only major championship Tom Watson hasn't won?

Chip Shot

As a boy Seve Ballesteros practiced all his shots with a 3-iron. He had no choice — it was his only club.

QUIZ ANSWER: The PGA Championship

AUGUST 28th

TODAY'S THOUGHT: "An amateur golfer is one who plays for honor — in my mind, that's tougher than playing for money."
—*Willie Turnesa, 1938 U.S. Amateur champion*

HISTORY: On this date in 1922 the United States defeated Great Britain and Ireland in the first official Walker Cup match, 8-4.

QUIZ: The 1995 U.S. Open was played at Shinnecock Hills GC. How many other Opens had the course hosted before that year?

Chip Shot

British writer Bernard Darwin, who came to America to cover the match, became a player and the team's captain.

QUIZ ANSWER: Two, in 1896 and 1986

AUGUST 29th

TODAY'S THOUGHT: "The players themselves can be classified roughly into two groups — the attractions and the entry fees." —*Jimmy Demaret, on the PGA Tour*

HISTORY: On this date in 1993 Brandie Burton made a birdie putt on the first playoff hole to win the rain-drenched duMaurier Classic.

QUIZ: What five Americans have won the British Open in consecutive years?

Chip Shot

The first African-American to tee it up at The Masters was Lee Elder, who missed the cut in 1975.

QUIZ ANSWER: Bobby Jones, Walter Hagen, Arnold Palmer, Lee Trevino and Tom Watson

AUGUST 30th

TODAY'S THOUGHT: "Women who seek equality with men lack ambition."
—*Bumper sticker on the back of Patty Sheenan's car*

HISTORY: On this date in 1992 Dottie Mochrie and Judy Dickinson battled for six playoff holes at the LPGA Challenge before Mochrie two-putted for par to win the tournament.

QUIZ: Who is second in LPGA tournament wins?

Chip Shot

The LPGA's low stroke average award is named after Glenna Collett Vare. In her debut, at the 1918 Rhode Island Championship, the 15-year old Vare finished dead last with a round of 132.

QUIZ ANSWER: Mickey Wright, who won 82

AUGUST 31st

TODAY'S THOUGHT: "All I know is that Nicklaus watches Hogan practice, and I never heard of Hogan watching Nicklaus practice." —*Tommy Bolt*

HISTORY: On this date in 1992 Justin Leonard won the U.S. Amateur Golf Championship, beating Thomas Sherrer, 8 & 7, at the Muirfield Village Golf Club.

QUIZ: Quick! Name the PGA Hall of Famer and 1954 U.S. Amateur champion who was born in Latrobe, Pennsylvania.

Chip Shot

Leonard's victory made him the third native Texan to win the title. The others were Billy Maxwell, in 1951 and Scott Verplank, in 1984.

QUIZ ANSWER: Arnold Palmer

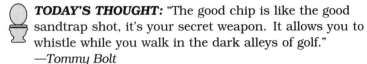

SEPTEMBER 1st

TODAY'S THOUGHT: "The good chip is like the good sandtrap shot, it's your secret weapon. It allows you to whistle while you walk in the dark alleys of golf."
—*Tommy Bolt*

HISTORY: On this date in 1946 Patty Berg won the first U.S. Women's Open.

QUIZ: In what decade did the entire PGA Tour prize money for a year reach a million dollars?

Chip Shot
LPGA players Betsy King, Beth Daniel, and Dottie Mochrie all attended Furman College in Greenville, SC.

QUIZ ANSWER: The 1950's — Prize money reached the one million dollar mark in 1958.

SEPTEMBER 2nd

TODAY'S THOUGHT: "The only shots you can be dead sure of are those you've had already." —*Byron Nelson*

HISTORY: On this date in 1940 Byron Nelson added another major to his list of victories, defeating Sam Snead in the finals of the PGA Championship. Nelson had already won The Masters and the U.S. Open in his career.

QUIZ: In the 1980's two golfers became U.S. Open champions by winning playoffs. Who were they?

Chip Shot
Nelson played in three consecutive finals at the PGA between 1939 and '41, but could win only one.

QUIZ ANSWER: Fuzzy Zoeller and Curtis Strange

SEPTEMBER 3rd

TODAY'S THOUGHT: "I would much rather be hitting the driver and a nine-iron out of the rough than hitting a driver and a four-iron out of the fairway."
—Jack Nicklaus

HISTORY: On this date in 1967 Kathy Whitworth won the LPGA Tour's richest event, edging Carol Mann at the Ladies' World Series of Golf.

QUIZ: Name the only foreign-born player to win the Vardon Trophy twice.

Chip Shot

Between 1971 and '83, Jack Nicklaus won the PGA Championship four times, finished in the top four on nine occasions, and was runner-up twice.

QUIZ ANSWER: Australian Bruce Crampton

SEPTEMBER 4th

TODAY'S THOUGHT: "A man who can putt is a match for anyone." *—Willie Park, Sr.*

HISTORY: On this date in 1932 Spaniard Olin Dutra won the PGA Championship for the first major of his career. Dutra went on to win the U.S. Open.

QUIZ: Tom Watson's 1977 British Open record of 268 was broken in 1993. Who did it?

Chip Shot

The first time Dr. Frank Stableford's scoring system was used was in 1932. Awarding points for performance against par was employed in a tournament near Liverpool, England.

QUIZ ANSWER: Greg Norman, with a 13-under-par 267

SEPTEMBER 5th

TODAY'S THOUGHT: "If you moved Pebble Beach fifty miles inland, no one would have heard of it."
—*Jimmy Demaret*

HISTORY: On this date in 1993 Billy Mayfair celebrated his first PGA Tour victory, winning the Greater Milwaukee Open.

QUIZ: Pebble Beach is one of three public courses to host the PGA Championship. Can you name the other two?

Chip Shot
PGA Tour player Lon Hinkle is a fifth cousin, once removed, of Abraham Lincoln.

QUIZ ANSWER: North Carolina's Tanglewood GC and Kemper Lakes GC in Illinois

SEPTEMBER 6th

TODAY'S THOUGHT: "A good player who is a great putter is a match for any golfer. A great hitter who cannot putt is a match for no one."
—*Ben Sayers, writer*

HISTORY: On this date in 1916 Ed Oliver was born. Known as "Porky" because of his generous girth, Oliver was never the bride at the majors but was a disappointed bridesmaid many times.

QUIZ: Who holds the record for appearing in the most Masters?

Chip Shot
Oliver and five other golfers were disqualified from the 1940 U.S. Open for starting before their scheduled tee time.

QUIZ ANSWER: Sam Snead, with 44

SEPTEMBER 7th

TODAY'S THOUGHT: "It's a lot easier hitting a quarterback than a little white ball."
—*Bubba Smith, actor and former football player*

HISTORY: On this date in 1923 Louise Suggs was born. A founder of the LPGA, Suggs was the first woman elected to the Hall of Fame in 1951.

QUIZ: This golfer's only victory in the 1950's was a memorable one. Who beat Ben Hogan in a playoff to win the 1955 U.S. Open?

Chip Shot
The shortest hole on the British Open rota is the eighth at Royal Troon, Scotland. It's 126 yards long.

QUIZ ANSWER: Jack Fleck

SEPTEMBER 8th

TODAY'S THOUGHT: "I used to think pressure was standing over a four-foot putt knowing I had to make it. I learned that real pressure was sixty-five people waiting for their food with only thirty minutes left on their lunch hour break."
—*Amy Alcott, on the pressure of waitressing*

HISTORY: On this date in 1974 JoAnne Carner captured the Dallas Civitan Open.

QUIZ: Mike Souchak won the 1955 Texas Open with a record 72-hole score. What did Souchak shoot?

Chip Shot
The greater the bet, the longer the short putts become.

QUIZ ANSWER: He had a 27-under-par 257.

SEPTEMBER 9th

TODAY'S THOUGHT: "Golf, especially championship golf, isn't supposed to be any fun, was never meant to be fair, and never will make any sense."
—*Charles Price, writer*

HISTORY: On this date in 1990 Patty Sheehan won the first of two straight tournaments when she took the Ping-Cellular One Golf Championship.

QUIZ: Who won the 1986 PGA Championship?

Chip Shot

After a pro-am at Doral in 1970, Raymond Floyd wrote his front-side score of 36 in the space reserved for the ninth hole. He signed the card and ended up with a round of 110.

QUIZ ANSWER: Bob Tway

SEPTEMBER 10th

TODAY'S THOUGHT: "His follow-through resembled a duck hunter tracking a teal."
—*Al Barkow, writer, on Arnold Palmer*

HISTORY: On this date in 1929 the commander-in-chief of Arnie's Army was born. Arnold Palmer would become the first golfer to win four Masters.

QUIZ: Legal or illegal? A candy wrapper is lying on my ball in the fairway. As I pick the wrapper up, my ball moves.

Chip Shot

The golfer who leads the PGA Tour in prize money for the season is awarded the Palmer Trophy.

QUIZ ANSWER: There is no penalty. A candy wrapper is not a natural object.

SEPTEMBER 11th

TODAY'S THOUGHT: "Golf is the 'only-est' sport."
—*Hale Irwin*

HISTORY: On this date in 1992 Raymond Floyd made his debut on the Senior PGA Tour at the Bank One Senior Golf Classic.

QUIZ: True or false? No Asian has ever won a major championship.

Chip Shot

Skip Kendall's week at the 1995 Nissan Open was a memorable one. On Monday, he crashed a tournament sponsor's courtesy car and escaped unscathed. That night, he awoke in pain from a toothache that needed root canal work. And, finally, Kendall shot a 183 to finish 46th in the tournament.

QUIZ ANSWER: True

SEPTEMBER 12th

TODAY'S THOUGHT: "Professional golf has become a game with too much character and not enough characters." —*Thomas Boswell, writer*

HISTORY: On this date in 1993 David Frost birdied the final hole for a one-stroke victory in the Canadian Open.

QUIZ: The "Augusta National Invitation Tournament" was the original name of what tournament?

Chip Shot

Joe Lucius is the golfer who scored 13 aces on the 15th hole at the Mohawk GC in Ohio. Lucius was nearly as successful on the 10th hole, which he aced 10 times.

QUIZ ANSWER: The Masters

SEPTEMBER 13th

TODAY'S THOUGHT: "The fun you get from golf is in direct ratio to the effort you don't put into it."
—*Bob Allen*

HISTORY: On this date in 1949 the Ladies Professional Golf Association was founded.

QUIZ: I'm making my charge at the PGA Championship when I ask you, my caddie, to hand me my "lofter". What club do you hand me?

Chip Shot

Clayton Heafner was known as a fiery competitor by his fellow pros. Just before Heafner was about to tee off at the 1941 Oakland (CA) Open, the marshal mispronounced his name. Insulted, Heafner withdrew from the tournament.

QUIZ ANSWER: My 8-iron

SEPTEMBER 14th

TODAY'S THOUGHT: "You don't go home and talk about the great tennis courts that you played but you do talk about the golf courses you played."
—*Hank Ketcham, cartoonist*

HISTORY: On this date in 1927 Gardner Dickinson was born. Dickinson was a member of U.S. Ryder Cup teams in 1967 and 1971.

QUIZ: Oakmont CC was the course where Johnny Miller fired a final round of 63 to win the 1973 U.S. Open. Where is it located?

Chip Shot

Winless in 18 years on the PGA Tour, Gary McCord had "NO WINS" on his vanity license plate.

QUIZ ANSWER: Oakmont, Pennsylvania

SEPTEMBER 15th

TODAY'S THOUGHT: "Show me someone who gets angry once in a while, and I'll show you a guy with a killer instinct. Show me a guy walking down the fairway smiling and I'll show you a loser." —*Lee Trevino*

HISTORY: On this date in 1899 Willie Smith won the fifth U.S. Open.

QUIZ: Tommy Armour won three of the four major championships in his career. What's the only tournament he didn't win?

Chip Shot

In 1899 golfers at the Atlantic City (NJ) CC came up with the word "birdie" when George Crump put his second shot inches from the hole after his ball hit a bird in flight.

QUIZ ANSWER: The Masters

SEPTEMBER 16th

TODAY'S THOUGHT: "Most golfers prepare for disaster. A good golfer prepares for success." —*Bob Toski*

HISTORY: On this date in 1961 21-year old Jack Nicklaus won his second U.S. Amateur title.

QUIZ: Name the native country of 1967 British Open champion Roberto deVicenzo.

Chip Shot

Because the golf course in Tientsin, China is laid out in a cemetery, greens are situated between grave mounds. Local rule: A ball which rolls into an open grave may be lifted without penalty.

QUIZ ANSWER: Argentina

SEPTEMBER 17th

 TODAY'S THOUGHT: "What other people may find in poetry or art museums, I find in the flight of a good drive." —*Arnold Palmer*

HISTORY: On this date in 1897 English pro Joe Lloyd became champion of the U.S. Open as foreign-born players continued to dominate.

QUIZ: When was the last time a golfer won the U.S. Open in his first attempt?

Chip Shot

The silver claret jug presented to the winner of the British Open is not kept by the champion, but is returned to the Royal & Ancient GC where it is displayed in the club's trophy case.

QUIZ ANSWER: 1913, when Francis Ouimet won

SEPTEMBER 18th

 TODAY'S THOUGHT: "Golf is, I should say offhand, the most useless outdoor game ever devised to waste the time and try the spirit of man."
—*Westbrook Pegler, writer*

HISTORY: On this date in 1994 the United States beat the International team, 20-12, to win the inaugural Presidents' Cup.

QUIZ: What's the last name of the LPGA player known by the first name "Muffin"?

Chip Shot

PGA Tour member Bruce Lietzke is actress Kirstie Alley's first cousin.

QUIZ ANSWER: Spencer-Devlin

SEPTEMBER 19th

TODAY'S THOUGHT: "The player may experiment about his swing, his grip, his stance. It is only when he begins asking his caddie's advice that he is getting on dangerous ground." —*Sir Walter Simpson, writer*

HISTORY: On this date in 1993 South African David Frost won his second straight tournament, defending his title at the Hardee's Golf Classic.

QUIZ: Name the only two golfers to successfully defend their Masters titles.

Chip Shot
Golf's richest first prize is at the Million Dollar Challenge in Sun City, South Africa. Low score gets $1 million.

QUIZ ANSWER: Jack Nicklaus, in 1966 and Nick Faldo, in 1990

SEPTEMBER 20th

TODAY'S THOUGHT: "Naturally, it was my hope to win out. I simply tried my best to keep this cup from going to our friends across the water."
—*Francis Ouimet, after the 1913 U.S. Open*

HISTORY: On this date in 1913 20-year old Francis Ouimet stunned British greats Harry Vardon and Ted Ray in a playoff to win the U.S. Open.

QUIZ: Who was the only foreign-born player to win the U.S. Open in the 1960's?

Chip Shot
Also making his Open debut was 20-year old Walter Hagen. He finished three strokes back.

QUIZ ANSWER: Gary Player, who won in 1965

SEPTEMBER 21st

TODAY'S THOUGHT: "It matters not the sacrifice which makes the duffer's wife so sore. I am the captive of my slice. I am the servant of my score."
—*Grantland Rice*

HISTORY: On this date in 1969 Donna Caponi won her second tournament of the year, edging Kathy Whitworth at the Lincoln-Mercury Open. Caponi's first win that year came at the U.S. Women's Open.

QUIZ: Name the first American 18-hole course.

Chip Shot

In 1969 Kathy Whitworth was a winner 7 times and finished second 7 times.

QUIZ ANSWER: The Chicago Golf Club, which opened in 1894

SEPTEMBER 22nd

TODAY'S THOUGHT: "My putter will not be flying first-class home with me." —*Nick Faldo*

HISTORY: On this date in 1905 Willie Anderson, the first dominant golfer in America this century, won his third straight, and fourth overall, U.S. Open.

QUIZ: This former PGA Championship winner was up to his knickers in money in 1993, winning over $900,000. Yet he didn't win a single tournament that year. Who was he?

Chip Shot

Costantino Rocco became the first Italian to play in the Ryder Cup when he played for Europe in 1993.

QUIZ ANSWER: Payne Stewart, who won $982,875 that year

The Bathroom Golf Almanac

SEPTEMBER 23rd

TODAY'S THOUGHT: "Great players win with their minds. They see nothing but positives out there." —*Chi Chi Rodriguez*

HISTORY: On this date in 1958 Larry Mize was born. Mize won the 1987 Masters with a 100-foot chip shot on the second hole of a playoff with Greg Norman.

QUIZ: Only three golfers have ever competed in over 30 consecutive U.S. Opens. Who are they?

Chip Shot
In 1981 Australian TV tycoon Kerry Parker hired PGA Tour pro Phil Rodgers for two weeks of private lessons. The fee, in addition to Rodgers' airfare, was $50,000.

QUIZ ANSWER: Gene Sarazen, Arnold Palmer and Jack Nicklaus

SEPTEMBER 24th

TODAY'S THOUGHT: "St. Andrews...crotchety and eccentric, but also elegant." —*Tony Lema*

HISTORY: On this date in 1895 Tommy Armour was born. The "Silver Scot" won the U.S. and British Opens despite having lost an eye in a mustard gas attack during World War I.

QUIZ: Bobby Jones won his native state's amateur title at the age of 14. Name the state.

Chip Shot
Armour's 1931 British Open win came at Carnoustie, the first Open to be played in his homeland, Scotland.

QUIZ ANSWER: Georgia

SEPTEMBER 25th

TODAY'S THOUGHT: "He is the reason we're playing for all this money today." —*Ken Still, on Arnold Palmer*

HISTORY: On this date in 1949 Louise Suggs won the U.S. Women's Open decisively, beating Babe Zaharias by 14 strokes. Suggs carded an opening round of 69 and finished with a record 291.

QUIZ: From 1897 until 1933 the NCAA golf team champions came from the same conference. Which one?

Chip Shot

Jack Nicklaus holds the record for the longest time between victories at The Masters. Nicklaus first won the tournament in 1963 and then again in 1986, a span of 23 years.

QUIZ ANSWER: The Ivy League, dominated by Yale

SEPTEMBER 26th

TODAY'S THOUGHT: "It's funny. You need a fantastic memory in this game to remember the great shots, and a very short memory to forget the bad ones."
—*Gary McCord*

HISTORY: On this date in 1925 Walter Hagen defended his PGA Championship title at the expense of Bill Mehlhorn, 6 & 5. It was Hagen's third title overall.

QUIZ: The course record at St. Andrews is 62, shot by this American during a match in the 1987 Dunhill Cup. Who was he?

Chip Shot

Mehlhorn knew he was in for a rough day when Hagen aced the first hole of the match.

QUIZ ANSWER: Curtis Strange, against Greg Norman

SEPTEMBER 27th

TODAY'S THOUGHT: "I have never felt so lonely as on a golf course in the midst of a championship with thousands of people around, especially when things began to go wrong and the crowd started wandering away." —*Bobby Jones*

HISTORY: On this date in 1930 Bobby Jones secured his place among golf's greats by winning the U.S. Amateur and completing the Grand Slam.

QUIZ: Name the native country of PGA Tour player T.C. Chen.

Chip Shot

Fittingly, Jones' win was at the Merion Cricket Club, the course where he had made his debut in the Amateur.

QUIZ ANSWER: Taiwan

SEPTEMBER 28th

TODAY'S THOUGHT: "Hell, this is only Wednesday. Nobody ever made money on Wednesday."
—*Jimmy Demaret, after a bad practice round*

HISTORY: On this date in 1921 Walter Hagen won the first of his five PGA Championships. Hagen beat Jim Barnes, that year's U.S. Open champ, 3 & 2.

QUIZ: When this golfer won the 1982 LPGA Championship, she became the first Australian to win an LPGA major. Who was she?

Chip Shot

Raymond Floyd was the first golfer to win on both the PGA Tour and the PGA Senior Tour in the same year, 1992.

QUIZ ANSWER: Jan Stephenson

SEPTEMBER 29th

TODAY'S THOUGHT: "An amateur golfer truly moves heaven and earth." —*Anonymous*

HISTORY: On this date in 1991 the U.S. ended Europe's six-year Ryder Cup reign when Bernhard Langer missed a 5-foot putt on the final hole. And, Pat Bradley came up a winner at the MBS LPGA Classic, her 30th career victory which qualified her for the LPGA Hall of Fame.

QUIZ: Who was the first American to win a PGA Championship?

Chip Shot
Two-time NCAA champion and 1987 U.S. Open winner, Scott Simpson, failed the PGA qualifying school twice.

QUIZ ANSWER: Walter Hagen, in 1921

SEPTEMBER 30th

TODAY'S THOUGHT: "Looking up is the biggest alibi ever invented to explain a terrible shot. By the time you look up, you've already made the mistake that caused the bad shot." —*Harvey Penick*

HISTORY: On this date in 1973 Sam Adams finished 16-under-par at the Quad Cities Open for his first victory on the PGA Tour. That tournament record held up for 15 years.

QUIZ: Name the youngest golfer to ever win The Masters.

Chip Shot
Don't you hate playing golf with a player so good, he doesn't have to cheat?

QUIZ ANSWER: Tiger Woods, at age 21, in 1997

OCTOBER 1st

TODAY'S THOUGHT: "The most advanced medical brains in the universe have yet to discover a way for a man to relax himself, and looking at a golf ball is not the cure." —*Milton Gross, writer*

HISTORY: On this date in 1939 George Archer was born. Wrist and back problems short-circuited Archer's PGA Tour career, but the 1969 Masters winner is one of the better golfers on the Senior PGA Tour.

QUIZ: Name the last golfer to successfully defend his U.S. Open title.

Chip Shot
The lowest round in U.S. Women's Open history was a 65 by Sally Little, but it's the only major Little has never won.

QUIZ ANSWER: Curtis Strange, in 1988 and '89

OCTOBER 2nd

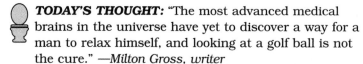

TODAY'S THOUGHT: "Let's face it, 95 percent of this game is mental. A guy plays lousy golf, he doesn't need a pro, he needs a shrink." —*Tom Murphy*

HISTORY: On this date in 1994 Larry Gilbert outdueled Raymond Floyd to win the Senior PGA Tour's Vantage Championship by one stroke. The former club pro shot three rounds of 66.

QUIZ: Since 1950, three players with exactly four letters in their last names have won the British Open. Who are they?

Chip Shot
Chick Evans, Jr. played in 50 consecutive U.S. Amateur Golf Championships. He won the title twice.

QUIZ ANSWER: Tomy Lema, Sandy Lyle and John Daly

OCTOBER 3rd

TODAY'S THOUGHT: "We really have to play with 15 clubs. We have 14 in our bag and the 15th in our head." —*Greg Twiggs, on the PGA Tour*

HISTORY: On this date in 1993 John Inman prevailed in a five-way playoff to win the Southern Open.

QUIZ: What Hall of Fame LPGA golfer is married to a baseball World Series MVP winner?

Chip Shot

Seve Ballesteros, when asked if he and Lee Trevino speak Spanish when they see each other, replied, "No, Trevino speaks Mexican."

QUIZ ANSWER: Nancy Lopez, who's married to Ray Knight

OCTOBER 4th

TODAY'S THOUGHT: "It's like playing in a straitjacket. They just lay you up on the rack and twist on both ends." —*Ben Crenshaw, on U.S. pressure*

HISTORY: On this date in 1895 ten professionals and an amateur competed in the first U.S. Open at the Newport (RI) GC.

QUIZ: Who is the only man to lose two playoffs and never win the U.S. Open?

Chip Shot

The inaugural Open had been postponed from September so it wouldn't clash with the America's Cup yacht races, which were held in Newport.

QUIZ ANSWER: Mike Brady lost playoffs in 1911 and '19.

OCTOBER 5th

TODAY'S THOUGHT: "In my opinion, you're a long time dead, so you might as well have fun while you can." —*Laura Davies*

HISTORY: On this date in 1900 Harry Vardon became the first foreign-based professional to win the U.S. Open. Vardon beat that year's British Open champ, J.H. Taylor, by two strokes at the Chicago GC.

QUIZ: Can you name the amateur golfer who has won the most British Open championships?

Chip Shot

Vardon was in the midst of an American tour when he played the Open. His itinerary covered 20,000 miles.

QUIZ ANSWER: Bobby Jones won in 1926, '27 and '30.

OCTOBER 6th

TODAY'S THOUGHT: "To succeed at anything, you must have a huge ego. I'm not talking about confidence. Confidence is self-assurance for a reason. Ego is self-assurance for no good reason."
—*Frank Beard*

HISTORY: On this date in 1928 Leo Diegel topped Al Espinosa, 6 & 5, to win the PGA Championship.

QUIZ: Byron Nelson holds the record for most victories in one year with 18 wins in 1945. Who's second?

Chip Shot

Leo Diegel's win in the 1928 PGA Championship ended Walter Hagen's unbeaten streak at 22 matches.

QUIZ ANSWER: In 1946 Ben Hogan won 13 tournaments.

OCTOBER 7th

TODAY'S THOUGHT: "Too many people carry the last shot with them. It is a heavy and useless burden." —*Johnny Miller*

HISTORY: On this date in 1965 Robert Mitura shot the ace of all aces with his 440-yard hole-in-one at the 10th hole of the aptly-named Miracle Hills GC in Omaha, Nebraska. Mitura was aided by a 50 mph wind.

QUIZ: What golfer was called "Mr. X" during his PGA Tour career?

Chip Shot

Gary Hallberg's hole-in-one in the third round of the 1995 U.S. Open was the 27th known ace in an Open.

QUIZ ANSWER: Miller Barber was dubbed "Mr. X" because of his fondness for solitude.

OCTOBER 8th

TODAY'S THOUGHT: "Jack Nicklaus has become a legend in his spare time." —*Chi Chi Rodriguez*

HISTORY: On this date in 1973 Jack Nicklaus won the $25,000 first prize at the Ohio-Kings Island Open. The Golden Bear donated the money to charity.

QUIZ: A three-time Masters champ, I appeared on the cover of "Golf" magazine's first issue in April, 1959. Who am I?

Chip Shot

To train Tommy Nakajima to play in the rain, his father used to squirt him in the face with a hose while the future pro hit golf balls.

QUIZ ANSWER: Jimmy Demaret

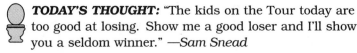

OCTOBER 9th

TODAY'S THOUGHT: "The kids on the Tour today are too good at losing. Show me a good loser and I'll show you a seldom winner." —*Sam Snead*

HISTORY: On this date in 1994 Rick Fehr joined the list of single-tournament winners when he captured the Walt Disney World Golf Classic. Only four golfers were able to win more than one event that year.

QUIZ: Name the English golfer who was the only foreign-born player to win the U.S. Open in the 1970's.

Chip Shot

Acording to the National Golf Foundation, the average 18-hole golf course covers 133 acres, half of which is rough.

QUIZ ANSWER: Tony Jacklin, who won in 1970

OCTOBER 10th

TODAY'S THOUGHT: "My game is not for display right now. I do, however, get great pleasure from playing and replaying holes in my mind."
—*Ben Hogan, on retirement*

HISTORY: On this date in 1962 Joseph Boydstone scored three holes-in-one on the front nine of his round at the Bakersfield (CA) GC course.

QUIZ: What country club hosted the first PGA Championship?

Chip Shot

At the 1992 Players Championship, John Daly dashed around the course in 1 hour, 49 minutes, carded an 80, and received a reprimand from the PGA Tour.

QUIZ ANSWER: Siwanoy CC in Bronxville, NY

OCTOBER 11th

TODAY'S THOUGHT: "Many shots are spoiled at the last instant by efforts to add a few more yards." —*Bobby Jones*

HISTORY: On this date in 1991 Chip Beck tied pro golf's all-time low score, shooting a 13-under-par 59 in the third round of the Las Vegas Invitational. Beck matched Al Geiberger's record-score with 13 birdies and 5 pars.

QUIZ: Legal or illegal? My ball is overhanging the lip of the cup and I wait two minutes. At that point, the ball falls into the cup.

Chip Shot
By breaking 60, Beck received a $1 million bonus.

QUIZ ANSWER: Illegal—one-stroke penalty

OCTOBER 12th

TODAY'S THOUGHT: "Some hotel rugs are impossible to putt." —*Tom Watson*

HISTORY: On this date in 1991 Chip Beck followed-up his record-matching 59 with a 68 in the fourth of five rounds in the Las Vegas Invitational.

QUIZ: What golf club is considered to be the oldest American golf club in continuous operation?

Chip Shot
Even though the USGA legalized steel-shafted clubs in 1924, Bobby Jones used hickory-shafted clubs through 1930.

QUIZ ANSWER: St. Andrews of Hastings-on-Hudson, NY was founded on November14, 1888.

OCTOBER 13th

TODAY'S THOUGHT: "I don't make mistakes. I make disasters." —*Bob Goalby*

HISTORY: On this date in 1963 Mickey Wright won the LPGA Championship for the fourth time in six years.

QUIZ: You remember Gene Sarazen's famous double-eagle in the 1935 Masters. Who was his playing partner that day?

Chip Shot

Arnold Palmer started the 1993 Masters with birdies on the first three holes, a first for the four-time champ. But he bogeyed five of the next six holes, finishing at 2-over 74.

QUIZ ANSWER: Sarazen was paired with Walter Hagen.

OCTOBER 14th

TODAY'S THOUGHT: "I owe a lot to my parents, especially my mother and father." —*Greg Norman*

HISTORY: On this date in 1984 Bernhard Langer birdied 10 of the first 15 holes at the Spanish Open on his way to a 10-under-par 62.

QUIZ: True or false? Kathy Whitworth, the career leader in wins on any tour with 88, never won the U.S. Women's Open.

Chip Shot

Golf is a lot like taxes. You drive hard to get to the green and then wind up in the hole.

QUIZ ANSWER: True

OCTOBER 15th

TODAY'S THOUGHT: "I know it's difficult to make it, but you've got to try it if you love golf and love the history of golf." —*Gary Hallberg, on qualifying for the British Open*

HISTORY: On this date in 1961 Mickey Wright finished ahead of Louise Suggs to win her second straight LPGA Championship.

QUIZ: The PGA Championship record score for 72 holes is 269. Name the golfer who did it in 1994.

Chip Shot
Wright and Suggs combined for 16 victories and 10 second-place finishes in the 25 tournaments on the LPGA tour.

QUIZ ANSWER: Nick Price, who finished 11-under-par

OCTOBER 16th

TODAY'S THOUGHT: "Hitting a golf ball correctly is the most sophisticated and complicated maneuver in all of sport, with the possible exception of eating a hot dog at a ball game without getting mustard on your shirt." —*Ray Fitzgerald, writer*

HISTORY: On this date in 1983 Lanny Wadkins tapped in a three-foot-putt as the United States won the Ryder Cup, 14-1/2 to 13-1/2.

QUIZ: Who's the oldest golfer to win a PGA Tour event?

Chip Shot
Golf is nature's way of making everyone a comedian.

QUIZ ANSWER: Sam Snead was 52 years old when he won the 1965 Greater Greensboro Open.

OCTOBER 17th

TODAY'S THOUGHT: "You can play a damned good shot there and find the ball in a damned bad place."
—George Duncan, British Open champ, on St. Andrews

HISTORY: On this date in 1860 eight golfers gathered at Prestwick GC to compete in the first British Open. Willie Park shot a 174 over three rounds of Prestwick's 12 holes.

QUIZ: Where did Greg Norman win his first British Open?

Chip Shot

First prize in the first British Open was a belt made of red leather adorned with silver plates.

QUIZ ANSWER: Turnberry, in Scotland, in 1986

OCTOBER 18th

TODAY'S THOUGHT: "Golf is a game whose aim is to hit a very small ball into an even smaller hole with weapons singularly ill-designed for the purpose."
—Sir Winston Churchill

HISTORY: On this date in 1992 England rode the momentum of an upset semi-final victory over the U.S. to beat Scotland and claim the Dunhill Cup International golf championship.

QUIZ: You putt your ball and it hits my caddie. What's the rule?

Chip Shot

When South African golfer Bobby Locke came to America in 1947, he won six of the 13 tournaments he entered.

QUIZ ANSWER: There is no penalty.

OCTOBER 19th

TODAY'S THOUGHT: "At my age, I don't even buy green bananas."
—*Lee Trevino, 47, at the 1987 British Open*

HISTORY: On this date in 1960 LPGA Tour player Dawn Coe-Jones was born. Coe-Jones was the 1983 Canadian Amateur champion and winner of the 1992 Women's Kemper Open.

QUIZ: It's the first round of The Players Championship. I ask you, my trusty caddie, to hand me my "mid mashie". What club do you hand me?

Chip Shot

When Hale Irwin travels, he takes along his regular set of clubs plus an extra driver, sand wedge and putter.

QUIZ ANSWER: My 3-iron

OCTOBER 20th

TODAY'S THOUGHT: "What's nice about our tour is you can't remember your bad shots."
—*Bobby Brue, on the Senior PGA Tour*

HISTORY: On this date in 1991 Seve Ballesteros equaled Gary Player's record of five World Match Play titles with a 3 & 2 victory over Nick Price.

QUIZ: How many holes were played in the shortest U.S. Open and in the longest?

Chip Shot

The PGA Tour record for fewest putts in a round is 18 held by Andy North, Kenny Knox, Mike McGee and Sam Trahan.

QUIZ ANSWER: The first three Opens were played at 36 holes. The 1931 Open took 144 holes because of two 36-hole playoffs.

OCTOBER 21st

TODAY'S THOUGHT: "Everybody has two swings: the one he uses during the last three holes of a tournament and the one he uses the rest of the time."
—*Toney Penna, pro golfer*

HISTORY: On this date in 1926 Bob Rosburg was born. Before turning to TV analysis, Rosburg followed up a second-place finish in the 1959 U.S. Open with a win in the PGA Championship.

QUIZ: Who's the oldest golfer to win The Masters?

Chip Shot

1959 was Bob Rosburg's year. Besides the PGA title, Rosburg needed only 19 putts in a round of the Pensacola Open.

QUIZ ANSWER: Jack Nicklaus, 46, in 1986

OCTOBER 22nd

TODAY'S THOUGHT: "Probably the worst hole on the course. Then again, being the worst hole at Pebble is like being the ugliest Miss America."
—*Rick Reilly, on the 11th hole at Pebble Beach*

HISTORY: On this date in 1961 Louise Suggs closed out the LPGA season with a win in the San Antonio Civitan. Suggs won 6 tournaments that year.

QUIZ: In what state is the Olympic Club, host to three U.S. Opens, located?

Chip Shot

Dallas amateur Doris Gray made 9 holes-in-one in 1982 at the Oak Cliff CC. She aced 3 different holes three times each.

QUIZ ANSWER: California

OCTOBER 23rd

TODAY'S THOUGHT: "Most people go on vacation twice a year to do what I do all the time. And they pay. I get paid." —*Chi Chi Rodriguez*

HISTORY: On this date in 1935 one of golf's leading ambassadors was born. Juan "Chi Chi" Rodriguez won 8 events on the PGA Tour before becoming the leading money-winner in the history of the Senior PGA Tour.

QUIZ: Name the only major won by Don January in his PGA Tour career.

Chip Shot

Just off the green but in thick grass is a good shot to practice. Using your putter, top the ball so it spins out of the grass and onto the green.

QUIZ ANSWER: The 1967 PGA Championship

OCTOBER 24th

TODAY'S THOUGHT: "Of all sports, golf least favors an excitable disposition." —*John Updike, writer*

HISTORY: On this date in 1993 Corey Pavin became the first American in 14 years to win the World Match Play Championship in England.

QUIZ: Two golfers have shot a record 271 to win The Masters. Who?

Chip Shot

Pavin's victory struck another blow for American golf after U.S. wins in the Ryder Cup and Dunhill Cup, both also on British soil.

QUIZ ANSWER: Jack Nicklaus, in 1965 and Raymond Floyd, in 1976

OCTOBER 25th

TODAY'S THOUGHT: "He took a swing like a man with a wasp under his shirt and his pants on fire, trying to impale a butterfly on the end of a scythe."
—*Paul Gallico, writer, on his playing partner*

HISTORY: On this date in 1992 Nick Price became the fourth $1 million winner of the season with a victory at the Texas Open.

QUIZ: Name the native country of British Open winner, Peter Thomson.

Chip Shot
North Carolinian Lang Martin once balanced seven golf balls vertically without any adhesive.

QUIZ ANSWER: Thomson, a five-time winner, was from Australia.

OCTOBER 26th

TODAY'S THOUGHT: "PGA West is what I call a one-time course. You play it to say you did and never play it again." —*Fuzzy Zoeller*

HISTORY: On this date in 1969 Carol Mann won her 8th tournament of the year despite shooting two-over-par at the Corpus Christi Civitan Open.

QUIZ: Five golf clubs were charter members of the USGA when it was founded in 1894. How many can you name?

Chip Shot
Carol Mann led the LPGA in earnings in 1969. Kathy Whitworth was the top money-winner the previous 4 years.

QUIZ ANSWER: St. Andrews GC, The Country Club, Shinnecock Hills GC, Newport GC and Chicago GC

OCTOBER 27th

TODAY'S THOUGHT: "You have to put your putter out to pasture every so often, let it eat and get fat so it can get more birdies." —*Greg Norman*

HISTORY: On this date in 1991 former NFL quarterback John Brodie scored his first victory on the Senior PGA Tour, beating Chi Chi Rodriguez and George Archer in a playoff at the Security Pacific Senior Classic.

QUIZ: Do you know the only golfer named Andy to win the U.S. Open?

Chip Shot

No golfer named Joe has ever won a major championship in this century.

QUIZ ANSWER: Andy North won it in 1978 and '85.

OCTOBER 28th

TODAY'S THOUGHT: "Remember, they were friends. For years they had shared each other's sorrows, joys, and golf balls, and sliced into the same bunkers." —*P.G. Wodehouse, "A Woman Is Only A Woman"*

HISTORY: On this date in 1972 JoAnn Prentice was the winner after ten holes of sudden death in the Corpus Christi Civitan, an LPGA playoff record.

QUIZ: Ben Hogan, in 1953, won all the majors except the PGA Championship. Why did Hogan have no chance to win the PGA?

Chip Shot

Golf is for backward executives: they talk nothing but golf in the office, and nothing but business on the links.

QUIZ ANSWER: It conflicted with the British Open.

OCTOBER 29th

TODAY'S THOUGHT: "Another weekend with nothing to do." *—Arnold Palmer, after missing a cut*

HISTORY: On this date in 1929 Gene Sarazen sank a hole-in-one in the first demonstration of night golf. A 400-million candlepower spotlight illuminated the course at the Briarcliff Manor GC in New York.

QUIZ: What golfer topped the annual money-winning list the most during the 1970's?

Chip Shot

The famous Old course at St. Andrews is actually a public golf course owned by the City of St. Andrews, Scotland

---

QUIZ ANSWER: Jack Nicklaus, 5 times

OCTOBER 30th

TODAY'S THOUGHT: "John Wayne gave up golf. How could a guy who won the West, recaptured Bataan and won the battle of Iwo Jima, let himself be defeated by a little hole in the ground?"
—James Edward Grant, screenwriter

HISTORY: On this date in 1994 Mark McCumber dropped a birdie putt on the first playoff hole to beat Fuzzy Zoeller in the Tour Championship.

QUIZ: Do you know what college Fuzzy Zoeller attended?

Chip Shot

Zoeller had five runner-up finishes that year, but it marked the first time he earned more than $1 million in a season.

QUIZ ANSWER: The University of Houston

OCTOBER 31st

TODAY'S THOUGHT: "Don't change the arc of your swing unless you are fairly sure you blundered in some way earlier." —*Red Lardner, writer*

HISTORY: On this date in 1991 the new, $2 million Tour Championship got underway on the No. 2 course at Pinehurst. John Daly birdied all the par-5 holes en route to a 3-under-par 68.

QUIZ: What was the name of the 1950's movie about Ben Hogan?

Chip Shot

When Poppy Hills replaced Cypress Point for the AT&T Pebble Beach National Pro-Am, Johnny Miller was heard to say, "It's like replacing Bo Derek with Roseanne Barr."

QUIZ ANSWER: "Follow the Sun", starring Glenn Ford

NOVEMBER 1st

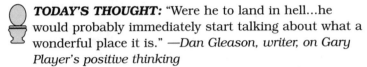

TODAY'S THOUGHT: "Were he to land in hell...he would probably immediately start talking about what a wonderful place it is." —*Dan Gleason, writer, on Gary Player's positive thinking*

HISTORY: On this date in 1935 Gary Player was born. The Hall-of-Famer is one of four golfers to have won all four major championships.

QUIZ: What's the only major championship Craig Stadler has won?

Chip Shot

When Player won the 1965 U.S. Open, he handed $25,000 of his $26,000 prize back to the USGA. $20,000 was to promote junior golf, $5,000 to fund cancer research.

QUIZ ANSWER: Stadler won The Masters in 1982.

NOVEMBER 2nd

TODAY'S THOUGHT:

"Golf is like bicycle shorts. It reveals a lot about people." —*Rick Reilly, writer*

HISTORY: On this date in 1941 Senior PGA Tour player Dave Stockton was born. Stockton was a two-time winner of the PGA Championship and captain of the 1991 Ryder Cup winning team.

QUIZ: A live bug is on your ball on the green. You mark your ball, pick it up, blow the bug off, and replace the ball. Is there any penalty?

Chip Shot

Stockton is a direct descendant of Richard Stockton, one of the signers of the Declaration of Independence.

QUIZ ANSWER: No

NOVEMBER 3rd

TODAY'S THOUGHT: "Golf is in the interest of good health and good manners. It promotes self-restraint and affords a chance to play the man and act the gentleman." —*President William Howard Taft*

HISTORY: On this date in 1976 Donna Caponi won the Mizuno Japan Classic for her third straight LPGA victory.

QUIZ: Who won the 1965 Masters by nine strokes?

Chip Shot

At the 1984 Memorial, Jack Nicklaus hit a tee shot that landed on the front porch of a nearby home. He hit a three-wood back to the fairway and finished with a bogey for the hole.

QUIZ ANSWER: Jack Nicklaus

NOVEMBER 4th

TODAY'S THOUGHT: "Golf puts a man's character on the anvil and his richest qualities—patience, poise, restraint—to the flame." —*Billy Casper*

HISTORY: On this date in 1973 Ben Crenshaw, playing in his first event as a PGA Tour member, won the San Antonio-Texas Open. Earlier in the year, Crenshaw was the winner in the Western Amateur.

QUIZ: Can you name the first player on the LPGA Tour from South Africa?

Chip Shot

The winner's trophy for The Masters is a silver replica of the clubhouse, with the champions' names inscribed on the base. A smaller version is awarded to each winner.

QUIZ ANSWER: Sally Little

NOVEMBER 5th

TODAY'S THOUGHT: "No one remembers who came in second." —*Walter Hagen*

HISTORY: On this date in 1927 Walter Hagen won the PGA Championship for the fourth time in a row.

QUIZ: What was unique about the winners of the four majors in 1994?

Chip Shot
Hagen defeated reigning U.S. Open champ, Tommy Armour, in a quarterfinal match.

QUIZ ANSWER: For the first time ever, none of the winners was an American. Jose Maria Olazabal of Spain won The Masters; Ernie Els of South Africa took the U.S. Open; and South African Nick Price won the British Open and the PGA Championship.

NOVEMBER 6th

TODAY'S THOUGHT: "We tournament golfers are much overrated. We get paid too much." —*Tom Watson*

HISTORY: On this date in 1994 Ernie Els made up a five-stroke deficit in six holes to win the inaugural Sarazen World Open Championship.

QUIZ: Of the following match play events, which is the oldest? Is it the? A: Solheim Cup B: Walker Cup C: Curtis Cup D: Ryder Cup

Chip Shot
Fred Daly remains the only Irishman to win a major championship. Daly sank a 30-foot putt on the last green to win the 1947 British Open by one stroke.

QUIZ ANSWER: B—The first Walker Cup was held in 1922.

NOVEMBER 7th

 TODAY'S THOUGHT: "Golf has drawbacks. It is possible, by too much of it, to destroy the mind."
—*Sir Walter Simpson, writer*

HISTORY: On this date in 1991 five-time British Open champion Tom Watson was named captain of the U.S. team for its 1993 Ryder Cup matches (which it would go on to win).

QUIZ: Who was the amateur from Arizona State who in 1991 won the PGA's Northern Telecom Tucson Open?

Chip Shot

In the 1950's, about 1,000 golf carts were in use. By the mid-60's, they numbered about 120,000. Today, there are more than 1,000,000.

QUIZ ANSWER: Phil Mickelson

NOVEMBER 8th

 TODAY'S THOUGHT: "I don't care to join any club that's prepared to have me as a member."
—*Groucho Marx*

HISTORY: On this date in 1964 Mickey Wright fired a record-setting 62 to win the Tall City Open in Midland, Texas. Wright came back from a ten-stroke deficit to beat Sherry Wheeler.

QUIZ: The only major title to elude Tom Watson is the PGA Championship. In 1978, he came close, losing in a playoff. Who beat him?

Chip Shot

The longest par-3 hole on the PGA tour is the 246-yard 13th at Dorall CC's Blue Course in Miami.

QUIZ ANSWER: John Mahaffey

NOVEMBER 9th

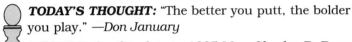

TODAY'S THOUGHT: "The better you putt, the bolder you play." —*Don January*

HISTORY: On this date in 1895 Mrs. Charles B. Brown won the first U.S. Women's Amateur Golf Championship. Brown shot 132 over 18 holes!

QUIZ: Three of the four golfers to defeat Greg Norman in major championship playoffs had the letter "z" in their last name. How many do you know?

Chip Shot

Neal Lancaster holds the record for the lowest nine hole score at a U.S. Open event, 29, in both 1995 and 1996.

QUIZ ANSWER: Fuzzy Zoeller, 1984 U.S. Open; Larry Mize, 1989 Masters; Mark Calcavecchia, 1989 British Open; Paul Azinger, 1993 PGA Championship

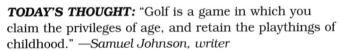

NOVEMBER 10th

TODAY'S THOUGHT: "Golf is a game in which you claim the privileges of age, and retain the playthings of childhood." —*Samuel Johnson, writer*

HISTORY: On this date in 1991 last-minute substitute Liselotte Neumann shot a 3-under-par 69 to win the LPGA's Mazda Japan Classic by two shots.

QUIZ: I won only three tournaments in my first 20 years on the PGA Tour. Two of them were at the U.S. Open. Who am I?

Chip Shot

Englishman John Ball won 8 British Amateur titles between 1888 and 1912.

QUIZ ANSWER: Andy North, who won the Open in 1978 and '85, and the Westchester Classic in 1977

NOVEMBER 11th

TODAY'S THOUGHT: "I love the game. It's all I am."
—*Dave Marr, TV analyst, on golf*

HISTORY: On this date in 1962 the United States won the Canada Cup for the third straight year. The team was led by Arnold Palmer and Sam Snead.

QUIZ: Name the golfer who holds the record for playing on the most United States Ryder Cup teams.

Chip Shot
Alcohol was prohibited in the U.S. from 1920 until 1933. Oddly, Americans won 12 of the 14 British Opens played during those years. After 1933, however, American golfers won only twice in the next 21 years.

QUIZ ANSWER: Billy Casper, who played in 8 Ryder Cups

NOVEMBER 12th

TODAY'S THOUGHT: "Any player can win a U.S. Open, but it takes a helluva player to win two."
—*Walter Hagen*

HISTORY: On this date in 1912 Ralph Guldahl was born. Guldahl became the fifth golfer to successfully defend his U.S. Open title when he won in 1938.

QUIZ: Between 1954 and 1958, Peter Thomson won 4 British Opens. In 1957, Thomson was runner-up. Who was the winner?

Chip Shot
Guldahl's first Open win in 1937 and his victory at The Masters came at the expense of Sam Snead who was runner-up both times.

QUIZ ANSWER: Bobby Locke of South Africa

NOVEMBER 13th

TODAY'S THOUGHT: "Golf is a better game played downhill." —*Jack Nicklaus*

HISTORY: On this date in 1994 the team of Fred Couples and Davis Love III set a tournament record by winning the World Cup of Golf for the third straight time. Their victory broke a mark set twice in the 1960's by Jack Nicklaus and Arnold Palmer.

QUIZ: What's the only major that Lee Trevino never won in his career?

Chip Shot

21 years after coming back from 7 strokes down to win the 1960 U.S. Open, Arnold Palmer came from 6 back after 36 holes to win the U.S. Senior Open.

QUIZ ANSWER: Trevino never won the Masters.

NOVEMBER 14th

TODAY'S THOUGHT: "The best perks of this office are who you get to play golf with. I've played with Jack Nicklaus, Arnold Palmer, Raymond Floyd, Amy Alcott." —*President Bill Clinton*

HISTORY: On this date in 1888 Scotsman John G. Reid became the founder of St. Andrews GC in Yonkers, NY, a 3-hole course.

QUIZ: Oak Hill CC was the site of Curtis Strange's 1989 U.S. Open victory. Where is the club located?

Chip Shot

Why is it that the golfer who tells his opponent it's only a game is the one who's winning?

QUIZ ANSWER: Rochester, NY

NOVEMBER 15th

TODAY'S THOUGHT: "It is impossible to imagine Goethe or Beethoven being good at billiards or golf."
—*H.L. Mencken, writer*

HISTORY: On this date in 1992 Davis Love III eagled the par-5 18th hole to break a tie with Mike Hulbert and win the Kapalua International by one stroke.

QUIZ: We're playing at Turnberry during the British Open when I ask you, my caddie, for my "brassie". What club do you give me?

Chip Shot
Love had finished second in the Kapalua International three times, including the previous year when Hulbert beat him in a playoff.

QUIZ ANSWER: My 2-wood

NOVEMBER 16th

TODAY'S THOUGHT: "The PGA Tour has lots of sheep, but Pavin is one of the wolves."
—*Johnny Miller, on Corey Pavin*

HISTORY: On this date in 1959 Corey Pavin was born. Pavin won the centennial U.S. Open in 1995 at Shinnecock Hills GC.

QUIZ: You've just shot a 4, but you wrote down a 3. What's the ruling?

Chip Shot
Conditions were so tough at the 1995 U.S. Open that 13 golfers, with 36 major titles between them, didn't make the cut. Pavin won with an even-par 280.

QUIZ ANSWER: Writing a lower score means disqualification from the tournament.

NOVEMBER 17th

TODAY'S THOUGHT: "Winners are a different breed of cat. They have an inner drive and are willing to give of themselves whatever it takes to win." —*Byron Nelson*

HISTORY: On this date in 1930 28-year old Bobby Jones announced his retirement from competitive golf.

QUIZ: Who is the oldest golfer to win a LPGA event?

Chip Shot

Jones would only come out of retirement to play in the Masters. He finished tied for 13th in the first tournament.

QUIZ ANSWER: JoAnne Carner was 46 when she won the Safeco Classic in 1985.

NOVEMBER 18th

TODAY'S THOUGHT: "It's just as hard to put yourself in there with a chance to win as it is to win."
—*Greg Norman, on trying to win a major*

HISTORY: On this date in 1901 Craig Wood was born. Wood ended years of frustration and second-place finishes when he won the 1941 Masters.

QUIZ: The first time total prize money at a U.S. Open exceeded $1,000 was in:

A: 1909   B: 1916   C: 1922   D: 1931

Chip Shot

Wood is one of two golfers to lose all four majors in playoffs. Wood lost the 1933 British Open, the 1934 PGA Championship, the 1935 Masters and the 1939 U.S. Open.

QUIZ ANSWER: B

NOVEMBER 19th

TODAY'S THOUGHT: "The mark of a champion is the ability to make the most of good luck and the best of bad." —*Anonymous*

HISTORY: On this date in 1942 Larry Gilbert was born. Gilbert joined the Senior PGA Tour in 1993 after years of success as a club pro.

QUIZ: In 1945, three golfers won 29 of the 35 events on the PGA tour. Who were they?

Chip Shot

Tommy Armour III needed an 8 on the final hole during the qualifying round of the 1983 TPC to make the cut. Armour hit three drives into the lake and ended play with a 9.

QUIZ ANSWER: Byron Nelson, Ben Hogan and Sam Snead

NOVEMBER 20th

TODAY'S THOUGHT: "For when the One Great Scorer comes to write against your name, He marks - not that you won or lost - but how you played the game." —*Grantland Rice*

HISTORY: On this date in 1993 28-year old Heather Farr, the youngest ever to qualify for the LPGA tour at age 20, lost her four-year battle with cancer.

QUIZ: Betsy King was the third golfer to enter the LPGA Hall of Fame in the 1990's. Who were the first two players?

Chip Shot

O.B. Keeler made the first transatlantic broadcast of a sporting event in 1930, reporting on the British Open.

QUIZ ANSWER: Pat Bradley and Patsy Sheehan

NOVEMBER 21st

TODAY'S THOUGHT: "Money was never a goal for me because of my amateur training. I was taught to win, and that was it." —*JoAnne Carner*

HISTORY: On this date in 1993 Raymond Floyd and Steve Elkington teamed up to win the $1.1 million Shark Shootout.

QUIZ: Hal Sutton has won one major in his career. Which one?

Chip Shot

In 1982, a radio station incorrectly reported that actor Victor Mature had died. Afterward, Mature said, "I'm the first dead man to make six double bogeys on the back nine on the day of his funeral."

QUIZ ANSWER: The 1983 PGA Championship

NOVEMBER 22nd

TODAY'S THOUGHT: "The major championships always comes down to the last nine holes. It takes character to win a major championship." —*Nick Price*

HISTORY: On this date in 1936 Englishman Densmore Shute defeated Jimmy Thomson, 3 & 2, to win the first of two straight PGA Championships.

QUIZ: Gene Sarazen's famous double eagle in the 1935 Masters traveled about 220 yards. What club did he use?

Chip Shot

Harry Vardon was the first athlete to sign an endorsement contract, promoting his ball, the Vardon Flyer.

QUIZ ANSWER: Sarazen used a 4-wood.

NOVEMBER 23rd

TODAY'S THOUGHT: "Here, Eddie, hold the flag while I putt out." —*Walter Hagen, to Edward, Prince of Wales*

HISTORY: On this date in 1985 50-year old rookie, Gary Player, won the Quadel Classic for his first victory on the Senior PGA Tour.

QUIZ: I joined the PGA Tour in 1987 and had at least one win in each of my first seven years. My first major was the PGA. Who am I?

Chip Shot
Because of the wartime rubber shortage, golf balls were in scarce supply in 1945. Sam Snead said he was paying $100 a dozen.

QUIZ ANSWER: Paul Azinger, who won the PGA in 1993

NOVEMBER 24th

TODAY'S THOUGHT: "I couldn't wait for the sun to come up the next morning so that I could get out on the course again." —*Ben Hogan*

HISTORY: On this date in 1991 Wayne Grady shot a final-round 69 for a three-stroke victory in the Australian PGA Championship.

QUIZ: In 1990, the first match play competition between the professional female golfers of the United States and Europe was held. What's the name of the tournament?

Chip Shot
Grady's previous win to the Australian victory was in the 1990 U.S. PGA Championship.

QUIZ ANSWER: The Solheim Cup

NOVEMBER 25th

TODAY'S THOUGHT: "A good golf course is like good music. It does not necessarily appeal the first time one plays it." —*Alister MacKenzie, golf course architect*

HISTORY: On this date in 1991 Pat Bradley was named LPGA Player of the Year for the second time in her career.

QUIZ: True or false? Pat Bradley has won every major on the LPGA Tour at least once in her career.

Chip Shot

When Shelley Hamlin won the 1992 Phar-Mor, she ended a record 14-year victory drought.

QUIZ ANSWER: True

NOVEMBER 26th

TODAY'S THOUGHT: "No power on earth will deter men from using a ball that will add to the length of their drive." —*"Golf Illustrated", 1902*

HISTORY: On this date in 1962 PGA Tour player, John Inman, was born. Inman turned pro in 1985 after a spectacular college career at North Carolina. In 1984, Inman was named College Player of the Year.

QUIZ: This tournament is sometimes called the "fifth major." What is it?

Chip Shot

When Ben Hogan returned home after winning the 1953 British Open, he was given a ticker-tape parade.

QUIZ ANSWER: The Tournament Players Championship

NOVEMBER 27th

 TODAY'S THOUGHT: "I'm aware that golf is probably some kind of mental disorder like gambling or women or politics." —*Dan Jenkins, writer*

HISTORY: On this date in 1994 Tom Watson topped a four-man field in the Skins Game with $210,000 in winnings.

QUIZ: Who's the only player to win two Masters playoffs?

Chip Shot

Golf made its national TV debut with the final round of the 1953 World Championship of Golf at Tam O'Shanter GC.

QUIZ ANSWER: Nick Faldo, who defeated Scott Hoch in 1989 and Raymond Floyd in 1990, both on the second hole of sudden death

NOVEMBER 28th

 TODAY'S THOUGHT: "Contrary to popular opinion, there are no sadistic motives behind how we set up a golf course for the U.S. Open."
—*David Eger, USGA senior director of rules*

HISTORY: On this date in 1992 Fred Couples had the best first day in the history of the Skins Game. Couples won six of nine skins to take home $130,000.

QUIZ: In 1987, this golfer became the first British woman to win the U.S. Open. Name her.

Chip Shot

The money Couples won that day boosted his winnings for the month to $652,000!

QUIZ ANSWER: Laura Davies

NOVEMBER 29th

TODAY'S THOUGHT: "Boy, it looked like a Rembrandt up there." —*Lee Trevino, on his shot that fell for an ace in the 1987 Skins Game*

HISTORY: On this date in 1992 Steve Elkington overcame wet and windy conditions to win the Australian Open.

QUIZ: What were the two majors Bobby Jones didn't win?

Chip Shot

When Tom Watson was asked how he helped the game of Gerald Ford, he replied, "First, hitting the ball. Second, finding it."

QUIZ ANSWER: The Masters and the PGA Championship

NOVEMBER 30th

TODAY'S THOUGHT: "I'm the best. I just haven't played yet." —*Muhammad Ali, on his golf game*

HISTORY: On this date in 1991 John Daly cleaned up in the first nine holes of the Skins Game, winning $120,000 and two automobiles.

QUIZ: What Australian won the U.S. Open during the 1980's?

Chip Shot

In the 1938 movie, "Carefree", Fred Astaire performed a dance solo in which he hit a row of golf balls while tap-dancing. The solo required almost 10 days of rehearsal and 2 days of filming. On screen, the dance lasted 3 minutes.

QUIZ ANSWER: David Graham, who won in 1981

DECEMBER 1st

TODAY'S THOUGHT: "There's no such thing as natural touch. Touch is something you create by hitting millions of golf balls." —*Lee Trevino*

HISTORY: On this date in 1939 Lee Trevino was born. Trevino burst onto the golf scene with a win over Jack Nicklaus in the 1968 U.S. Open. The Hall-of-Famer has won 6 major championships in his career.

QUIZ: Englishman Ted Ray won the U.S. Open in 1920. The next Englishman to win did so exactly 50 years later. Who?

Chip Shot
In '68, Trevino became the first golfer in U.S. Open history to shoot less than 70 in all four rounds.

QUIZ ANSWER: Tony Jacklin

DECEMBER 2nd

TODAY'S THOUGHT: "Golf is a science, the study of a lifetime, in which you can exhaust yourself but never your subject." —*David Forgan, writer*

HISTORY: On this date in 1953 PGA Tour player Jay Haas was born. An NCAA champ and All-American at Wake Forest, Haas has quietly crossed the $4 million mark in earnings.

QUIZ: In 1993, Greg Norman became the first British Open champion to break 70 in all four rounds of the tournament. But he wasn't the first golfer to do it. Who was?

Chip Shot
Haas is the nephew of 1968 Masters champion Bob Goalby.

QUIZ ANSWER: Ernie Els, who finished tied for sixth

DECEMBER 3rd

TODAY'S THOUGHT: "Nicklaus loved the pressure. Palmer loved it. They not only loved it, they rose to another level, while guys like me were seeking a level below, just trying to get out of there." —*Frank Beard*

HISTORY: On this date in 1972 Jack Nicklaus captured the Walt Disney World Open to become the first golfer to win more than $300,000 in a season.

QUIZ: When Jack Nicklaus won his sixth Masters, in 1986, who was his caddie?

Chip Shot

In 1973, one year later, Nicklaus won the same tournament. With the win, he became the first golfer to earn more than $2 million in his career.

QUIZ ANSWER: Jack, Jr., his youngest son

DECEMBER 4th

TODAY'S THOUGHT: "I regard golf as an expensive way of playing marbles." —*G.K. Chesterton, writer*

HISTORY: On this date in 1994 Nick Faldo held off Nick Price and Ernie Els to win the Million Dollar Challenge by three shots.

QUIZ: Jerry Pate, Nick Price, Doug Weaver, and Mark Wiebe did something at the 1989 U.S. Open which had been done only 17 times in its history. What was it?

Chip Shot

Faldo was a runner-up three times in the Million Dollar Challenge, played in Sun City, South Africa.

QUIZ ANSWER: The four golfers each shot a hole-in-one.

DECEMBER 5th

TODAY'S THOUGHT: "The difference between me and an amateur is that I'm not afraid to screw up."
—*Fuzzy Zoeller*

HISTORY: On this date in 1993 Curtis Strange ended a four-year victory drought with a win in the Greg Norman Classic in Sydney, Australia.

QUIZ: Give the order of the four majors.

Chip Shot
There was no June swoon for Greg Norman in 1995. Playing in four tournaments, Norman earned $781,780 for the month.

QUIZ ANSWER: The Masters in April, the U.S. Open in June, the British Open in July, and the PGA Championship in August

DECEMBER 6th

TODAY'S THOUGHT: "In those days, the money was the main thing, the only thing I played for. Championships were something to grow old with."
—*Byron Nelson*

HISTORY: On this date in 1992 David Frost became the first three-time winner of the Million Dollar Challenge.

QUIZ: True or false? The British Amateur began before the British Open.

Chip Shot
Babe Zaharias was a great all-around athlete. Asked if there was anything she didn't play, she replied, "Yeah, dolls."

QUIZ ANSWER: False. The Amateur began in 1885, 25 years after the first professional Open.

DECEMBER 7th

TODAY'S THOUGHT: "Golf seems to me an arduous way to go for a walk. I prefer to take the dogs out."
—*Princess Anne of England*

HISTORY: On this date in 1929 Leo Diegel won his second straight PGA Championship with a 6 & 4 win over Johnny Farrell.

QUIZ: How come Bobby Jones never played in the Ryder Cup?

Chip Shot
The 1929 PGA was the first major championship to be played in California. The matches were held at the Hillcrest CC in Los Angeles.

QUIZ ANSWER: Jones was an amateur. The Ryder Cup is for professionals.

DECEMBER 8th

TODAY'S THOUGHT: "His future is ahead of him."
—*Steve Melnyk, on the prospects of Phil Mickelson*

HISTORY: On this date in 1991 Billy Andrade and Kris Tschetter parred the second playoff hole to win the J.C. Penney Classic.

QUIZ: Can you name the four rookies on the PGA Tour who can claim majors as their first victories?

Chip Shot
At 7,252 yards, the links at Carnoustie is the longest course ever played in British Open competition.

QUIZ ANSWER: Jack Nicklaus, '62 U.S. Open; Jerry Pate, '76 U.S. Open; John Daly, '91 PGA; and Ernie Els, '94 U.S. Open

DECEMBER 9th

TODAY'S THOUGHT: "It's an awfully empty life hitting golf balls every day. You are not giving much service."
—*Willie Auchterlonie, 1893 British Open champ*

HISTORY: On this date in 1991 John Daly won the Charles Bartlett Award for charitable contributions. Daly used money from his PGA Championship prize to start a scholarship fund for the daughters of a spectator killed by lightning during the championship.

QUIZ: What three golfers have won the British Open in three different decades?

Chip Shot
Samuel Ryder (Ryder Cup) didn't play golf until he was 50.

QUIZ ANSWER: Harry Vardon, J.H. Taylor and Gary Player

DECEMBER 10th

TODAY'S THOUGHT: "Golf is the cruelest of sports. Like life, it's unfair. It's a harlot. A trollop. It leads you on. It never lives up to its promises. It's not a sport, it's bondage. An obsession. A boulevard of broken dreams. It plays with men. And runs off with the butcher."
—*Jim Murray, writer*

HISTORY: On this date in 1937 Senior PGA Tour player Don Bies was born. Bies played the PGA Tour for 13 years, winning once.

QUIZ: What PGA Tour player is known as the "Zinger"?

Chip Shot
The easiest shot in golf is your fourth putt.

QUIZ ANSWER: Paul Azinger

DECEMBER 11th

TODAY'S THOUGHT: "All good players have good hands. And I'm afraid you have to be born with them." —*Dave Stockton*

HISTORY: On this date in 1991 the NY State Court of Appeals ruled that a golfer whose tee shot struck a moving car could not be sued for the resulting traffic accident. The golfer had watched as his shot sailed off the course and shattered a car's windshield.

QUIZ: It's called the "Saturday Slam". What is it?

Chip Shot
Golfer's prayer: May I live long enough to shoot my age.

QUIZ ANSWER: You've won the "Saturday Slam" after leading all of the majors after three rounds, a la Greg Norman in 1986.

DECEMBER 12th

TODAY'S THOUGHT: "Watch their eyes. Fear shows up when there is an enlargement of the pupils. Big pupils lead to big scores." —*Sam Snead*

HISTORY: On this date in 1899 George Grant received a patent for the golf tee. It came a year after a patent was granted for a rubber-cored golf ball.

QUIZ: In 1989, Mark Calcavecchia became the first American to win the British Open in six years. But he had to beat two Australians in a playoff to win the silver jug. Who were they?

Chip Shot
Shinnecock Hills GC was the first golf club in the nation to have a clubhouse. It was built in 1892.

QUIZ ANSWER: Wayne Grady and Greg Norman

DECEMBER 13th

TODAY'S THOUGHT: "The Ryder Cup is not only about winning, but also about goodwill. There is too little tradition left in the game as it is."
—*Dave Marr, U.S. captain in 1981*

HISTORY: On this date in 1992 Raymond Floyd won in convincing fashion in the Senior Tour Championship with a final round 7-under-par 65.

QUIZ: The oldest player ever to compete in the Ryder Cup sank the winning putt for the United States at the Belfry in 1993. Who?

Chip Shot

Three of the world's greatest golf courses—Royal Melbourne, Muirfield, and Olympic—have no water hazards.

QUIZ ANSWER: 51-year old Raymond Floyd

DECEMBER 14th

TODAY'S THOUGHT: "Ian Woosnam, you're from Wales. Is that a village in England?"
—*Reporter, at the 1991 Masters*

HISTORY: On this date in 1955 LPGA Tour player Jane Crafter was born. A pharmacist before joining the Tour, it was only appropriate that the Australian won the 1990 Phar-Mor at Inverarry.

QUIZ: What is the biggest possible margin in 18 holes of match play?

Chip Shot

More golf is shown at The Masters than any other televised event. Only four minutes of commercials per hour are allowed by Masters officials.

QUIZ ANSWER: 10 & 8

DECEMBER 15th

TODAY'S THOUGHT: "The only problem with the Senior Tour is that when you're through here, they put you in a box." —*J.C. Snead*

HISTORY: On this date in 1991 Mike Hill won the Senior Tour Championship to become the leading money-winner on the Senior PGA Tour.

QUIZ: Why didn't Nick Faldo receive the green jacket from the defending champion after his 1990 Masters victory?

Chip Shot

The first woman to write a book about golf was Mrs. Edward Kennard. In 1896, she wrote "The Sorrows of a Golfer's Wife".

QUIZ ANSWER: Faldo was the defending champion.

DECEMBER 16th

TODAY'S THOUGHT: "A match against Bobby Jones is just as though you got your hand caught in a buzz saw." —*Francis Ouimet, 1913 U.S. Open champion*

HISTORY: On this date in 1930 Bobby Jones received the first Sullivan Award as the nation's outstanding amateur athlete.

QUIZ: My real first names are Alexander Walter Barr, but you call me "Sandy". Who am I?

Chip Shot

Only 4 of the USGA's 13 national championships are decided at stroke play—the U.S. Open, the U.S. Women's Open, the U.S. Senior Open and the U.S. Senior Women's Amateur Championship.

QUIZ ANSWER: Sandy Lyle

DECEMBER 17th

TODAY'S THOUGHT: "In golf, humiliations are the essence of the game." —*Alistair Cooke, writer*

HISTORY: On this date in 1962 PGA Tour player Rocco Mediate was born. Mediate, who didn't get his first set of clubs until he was 16, had 6 top-10 finishes in his first 7 starts in 1991.

QUIZ: Has PGA tour player Jeff Sluman ever won a major championship?

Chip Shot
The last tournament Ben Hogan played in was the 1971 Houston Champion International.

QUIZ ANSWER: Yes. Sluman won the 1988 PGA Championship.

DECEMBER 18th

TODAY'S THOUGHT: "We were lucky we had (Bobby) Jones for so long, for he had a rare gift for passing ideas and ideals on to other people."
—*Herbert Warren Wind, writer*

HISTORY: On this date in 1971 golf lost one of its true heroes when Bobby Jones died. A stylish player, Jones qualified for every event he entered.

QUIZ: Two of Europe's top golfers have exactly 11 letters in their surnames. One of them is Seve Ballesteros. Can you name the other golfer?

Chip Shot
To put the career of Bobby Jones in perspective, only one amateur has won the U.S. Open since his 1930 retirement.

QUIZ ANSWER: Colin Montgomerie of Scotland

DECEMBER 19th

TODAY'S THOUGHT: "Once the golfing champion allows himself to suspect that playing a superb round is not the be-all and end-all of life, he is lost."
—*Anonymous*

HISTORY: On this date in 1993 Larry Mize dusted the field at the Johnny Walker Championship, finishing ten strokes ahead of runner-up Fred Couples.

QUIZ: Bernhard Langer of Germany has won the same major twice in his career. Which one?

Chip Shot

The famed Baltusrol GC raised livestock to fight the meat shortage during World War II.

QUIZ ANSWER: The Masters, in 1985 and 1993

DECEMBER 20th

TODAY'S THOUGHT: "You have the hands, now play with your heart."
—*Roberto deVicenzo, to Seve Ballesteros*

HISTORY: On this date in 1992 Nick Faldo birdied the last hole to force a playoff with Greg Norman in the World Championship. Faldo won the playoff.

QUIZ: What golfer holds the record for the U.S. Women's Open best score?

Chip Shot

The first tournament Lee Trevino won as a professional was the 1965 Texas State Open.

QUIZ ANSWER: Annika Sorenstam, who shot an 8-under-par 272 at Southern Pines, NC in 1996

DECEMBER 21st

TODAY'S THOUGHT: "The Rockies may crumble, Gibraltar may tumble, but St. Andrews isn't going anywhere."
—*Frank Deford, writer, on the famed Scottish course*

HISTORY: On this date in 1892 one of the game's all-time greats, Walter Hagen, was born. Hagen played hard on and off the course, winning 40 titles in his career including all four majors at least once.

QUIZ: True or false? Chi Chi Rodriguez has never won a major in his career.

Chip Shot

In 1922, Hagen became the first golf professional to manufacture golf clubs under his own name.

QUIZ ANSWER: True

DECEMBER 22nd

TODAY'S THOUGHT: "Golf is life. If you can't take golf, you can't take life." —*Anonymous*

HISTORY: On this date in 1894 the Amateur Golf Association of the United States was formed in New York. Later changed to the United States Golf Association, its purpose is to promote and conserve the best interests and true spirit of the game of golf.

QUIZ: What do you call a golfer with a zero handicap, other than good?

Chip Shot

Jan Stephenson was the first woman golf pro to design golf courses.

QUIZ ANSWER: A scratch golfer

DECEMBER 23rd

TODAY'S THOUGHT: "Arnold Palmer usually walks to the first tee quite unlike any other pro on the circuit. He doesn't walk onto it so much as climb into it, almost as though it were a prize ring."
—*Charles Price, writer*

HISTORY: On this date in 1928 Horton Smith won the Catalina Open with a four-round total of 245.

QUIZ: If he plays the Open at St. Andrews in the year 2000, it will be the 46th Open championship at which he's competed. Who is it?

Chip Shot

Jimmy Thompson wowed the galleries during the 1935 U.S. Open when he reached the 621-yard 12th green in two.

QUIZ ANSWER: Gary Player

DECEMBER 24th

TODAY'S THOUGHT: "I play with friends, but we don't play friendly games." —*Ben Hogan*

HISTORY: On this date in 1861 the first notable English amateur golfer, John Ball, Jr., was born. Ball ended thirty years of domination by Scottish pros when he won the British Open in 1890.

QUIZ: In the 1980's Europeans won The Masters five times. Can you name the four different players?

Chip Shot

Ben Hogan is the only player to have lost two Masters playoffs.

QUIZ ANSWER: Seve Ballesteros won in 1980 and '83; Bernhard Langer won in 1985; Sandy Lyle in 1988; and Nick Faldo in 1989.

DECEMBER 25th

TODAY'S THOUGHT: "The man who can approach does not need to putt."
—*J.H. Taylor, five-time British Open champion*

HISTORY: On this date in 1875 the youngest winner of the British Open, Tom Morris, Jr., died at the age of 24. Morris captured the Open title in 1868 when he was 18 years old.

QUIZ: This golfer played on two U.S. Walker Cup teams, in 1959 and '61, winning all four matches he played. Name him.

Chip Shot
Besides being the youngest to win the British Open, Morris is also the only golfer to win it four straight times.

QUIZ ANSWER: Jack Nicklaus

DECEMBER 26th

TODAY'S THOUGHT: "Winged Foot has the toughest eighteen finishing holes in golf." —*Dave Marr*

HISTORY: On this date in 1993 Jack Nicklaus, Raymond Floyd and Chi Chi Rodriguez teamed up to represent the PGA Senior Tour and won the Wendy's Three-Tour Challenge.

QUIZ: In the 19th century, most golf shafts were made of wood. What type of wood?

Chip Shot
Television didn't impress Horton Smith. Smith, president of the PGA from 1952-54, called it "a gimmick that wouldn't last".

QUIZ ANSWER: Hickory

DECEMBER 27th

TODAY'S THOUGHT: "I am the handicap in golf."
—*Boris Becker, tennis pro*

HISTORY: On this date in 1962 Sherri Steinhauer was born. Steinhauer's first victory on the Tour was a major one, coming at the 1992 duMaurier Classic.

QUIZ: How many European golfers have won the PGA Championship?

Chip Shot

Before teeing up for the 1919 U.S. Open playoff, Walter Hagen told opponent Mike Brady to roll down his sleeves. When asked why, Hagen replied, "So the gallery won't see your arms shaking." Hagen won the playoff by one stroke.

QUIZ ANSWER: None

DECEMBER 28th

TODAY'S THOUGHT: "Golf is the only game in which a precise knowledge of the rules can earn one a reputation for bad sportsmanship."
—*Patrick Campbell, writer*

HISTORY: On this date in 1946 Hubert Green was born. Green had 19 PGA Tour victories and was the winner of the 1977 U.S. Open as well as the 1985 PGA Championship.

QUIZ: What course played host to the first 12 British Opens?

Chip Shot

Arnold Palmer was the first British Open champion to shoot three rounds under 70. He did it in 1962.

QUIZ ANSWER: Prestwick, in Ayrshire, Scotland

DECEMBER 29th

TODAY'S THOUGHT: "Through the ball we are all the same. We just have different ways of getting it there." —*Charles Coody*

HISTORY: On this date in 1892 a 4-acre apple orchard became the new home of the St. Andrews Club.

QUIZ: In 1980, he wrote "The Rules of Golf, Explained and Illustrated". Three months later, he was penalized two shots for giving a tip during play. Name him.

Chip Shot

Use your putter if the fringe near the green is smooth and flat.

QUIZ ANSWER: Tom Watson

DECEMBER 30th

TODAY'S THOUGHT: "Golf is mostly a game of failures." —*Tommy Aaron*

HISTORY: On this date in 1975 Tiger Woods was born. Woods became the youngest champion of The Masters when he won the title in 1997.

QUIZ: Name the only player to score a double eagle at the U.S. Open.

Chip Shot

In the first 100 years of the U.S. Open, 31 tournaments were decided by playoffs. That's more than double the number of any other major championship.

QUIZ ANSWER: T.C. Chen did it at a par-5 hole at the 1985 Open at Oakland Hills CC.

DECEMBER 31st

TODAY'S THOUGHT: "It is almost impossible to remember how tragic a place the world is when one is playing golf." —*Robert Lynd, sociologist*

HISTORY: On this date in 1936 the USGA announced that, effective January 1, 1938, no more than 14 clubs would be allowed in tournament play.

QUIZ: An amateur has finished second at The Masters three times. Ken Venturi was the runner-up in 1956. Do you know the other two?

Chip Shot

The first American golf book was published in 1895. It was written by James Lee and titled, simply, "Golf in America".

QUIZ ANSWER: Frank Stranahan, in 1947 and Charlie Coe, in 1961